AUTOMATION AND NETWORKING OF LIBRARIES

AUTOMATION AND NETWORKING OF LIBRARIES

A MANUAL OF LIBRARY MANAGEMENT SOFTWARE AND APPLICATIONS OF COMPUTER TECHNOLOGY IN LIBRARIES

LakshmiKant Mishra
M.L.I.Sc., M.A., L.L.B., C.L.C., NET (UGC)
LIBRARIAN
Lucknow College of Architecture, Lucknow

Vishnu Srivastava
M.L.I.Sc., M.A., L.L.B., C.L.C., P.G.D.C.A., NET (UGC)
Asst. LIBRARIAN
High Court of Judicature, Allahabad

PUBLISHING FOR ONE WORLD

NEW AGE INTERNATIONAL (P) LIMITED, PUBLISHERS

New Delhi • Bangalore • Chennai • Cochin • Guwahati • Hyderabad
Jalandhar • Kolkata • Lucknow • Mumbai • Ranchi

Visit us at **www.newagepublishers.com**

Published by New Age International (P) Ltd., Publishers
First Edition: 2008

ISBN–(13) : 978-81-224-2234-4

ISBN–(10) : 81-224-2234-9

Rs. 280.00

C-08-01-2189

Printed in India at Ram Printograph, Delhi
Typeset in-house

PUBLISHING FOR ONE WORLD

NEW AGE INTERNATIONAL (P) LIMITED, PUBLISHERS
4835/24, Ansari Road, Daryaganj, New Delhi - 110002
Visit us at **www.newagepublishers.com**

"if you give a man a fish
he will have single meal,
if you teach him how to fish
he will eat all his life."

—*Old Chinese Proverb*

PREFACE

Automation is a technique and Computer is a tool. If you try to avoid it, the tool is useless. But if you learn how to use it, you will immediately understand that it is the most powerful and useful tool for information sharing and knowledge networking work that man has ever developed.

Libraries and Information Centres acquire, store and disseminate information, produced, sought for and processed by the human mind nowhere has the impact of the computer been greater than in the field of Library and Information Science. Information is a catalyst in the socio-economic, scientific, technological and cultural development of the society. Development in these fields of human activity leads to creation of new information related to that and also new and more efficient information storage media. This in terms contributes to further developments and multiplication of information. The present information explosion has literally drowned the libraries in an ocean of printed materials. In future awaits even greater threat and it is clear that libraries no more can function efficiently without computers which only can collect, process, store, retrieve and disseminate quickly and efficiently the required information from the present infinite quantum of information that exists. So computers will have to come and stay forever in all libraries and information centers that are to be live and efficient here in after.

The development in information technology has brought drastic changes in the way in which information is collected, stored, retrieved and distributed. A number of existing specialized databases, online information services, resource sharing networks and databases in CD-ROM necessitate the application of computers if libraries are to harness the possibilities offered by these developments. Libraries are becoming a blend of traditional collection along with an array of electronic storage and networking devices and terminals to serve as a switching centre or interface for outside information. The libraries and information centers that cannot adjust to these developments will not survive today as well as coming days. But the new technology in computers and data communication has simultaneously made library and information work more technical and complex than ever before. No longer, it is possible however, to learn these subjects entirely by specialists. It is only by an understanding of the basic concepts of computer technology that it will be possible to take full advantages of the opportunities available. Certainly no library and information professional can consider him to be fully prepared for the challenges of the forthcoming years without a through grounding of the computer and information systems, their techniques, equipments and practice.

Now, so many library management software packages and networking technologies are available in India for the information retrieval and storage as well as handling of all activities of libraries through computers. But still no any such work has been done to describe the limitations and merits of such software packages. During our work in various special libraries, we have tried few software packages viz. DBMS, (FoxPro), CLMS, CDS/ISIS, WINISIS, LIBSys etc. for computerisation of library activities.

Apart from that we are highly indebted to a number of authors from whom I have cited and got it prepared to present this work for the benefit of working library professionals in general and the students of study programmes in Library and Information Science in particular. This book has been especially written to comply with the syllabi and scope prescribed by the Library and Information Science Departments of various universities and institutions.

The most glaring feature of this book is the additional information on few concepts viz. Library Management Software Packages, Digital and Virtual Libraries, Status of Indian Library Network closely related to Library and Information Science subject.

We are deeply indebted to various sources of information from a number of standard references, journals and articles used purely for the updating of relevant data especially to websites of UNESCO, OCLC, UGC, NIC, DELNET, CALIBNET, LUCKLIBNET, INFORMATICS INDIA, INFO LIBRARIAN, and LIBSYS etc.

Suggestions for improvement are welcome.

LakshmiKant Mishra
Vishnu Srivastava

CONTENTS

CHAPTER 1

INTRODUCTION TO COMPUTER

Computers are affecting our lives in one way or the other. Government agencies such as airline and railway reservations, telephone and electricity bills, banking, medical diagnoses, weather forecasts and other organizations make use of computers in a variety of activities such as data processing and Management Information Systems (MIS). The list of services using computers is almost endless.

The library and information profession has also become aware of the potential of computer as a powerful tool, which can be utilized to improve both the operational efficiency of library and information personnel, and the quality and range of services provided to the user community.

1.1 MEANING AND DEFINITION

Historically speaking, the word computer has been derived from the Latin word 'computare' which means to calculate. This does not mean that a computer is just a calculator doing mathematical operations because nowadays 80 percent of the work done by a computer is non-mathematical. The word computer according to the Oxford English Dictionary is "an automatic electronic apparatus for making calculations or controlling operations that are expressible in numerical or logical terms. A computer can store, process and retrieve data as and when desired, so many people started calling it "data processor."

Actually it is an electronic device by which we perform arithmetic as well as logical operations (calculation & textual works). Abbreviation of COMPUTER denotes as follows-

C Common
O Operating
M Machine
P Particularly
U Used for

T Trade
E Education
R Research

1.2 HISTORICAL PERSPECTIVE

Although, the term computer as understood today is a relatively recent innovation, its development rests on centuries of research. Later as early as 1600 machines to perform arithmetic operations were developed by Pascal and Leibnitz and such efforts continued over the years, each effort leading to the betterment and perfection of the calculating machines. Ever since his existence man has been inventing and devising tools and techniques to aid him. In the primitive ages, he used his fingers for counting. When the need arose, he made use of pebbles, beads, seashells, stones and the like to keep an account of large numbers. As his necessities increased further he invented newer and newer devices. The Chinese are known to have devised **abacus** around 600 BC. An abacus is a clay board with a number of grooves in this pebbles are placed. These pebbles can be moved from side to side for the purpose of counting. Later on the material use changed, but the basic principle has remained the same. The abacus now has several rows of beads strung on wires in a rectangular frame. It helps in counting in the decimal system.

The **first machine** employing concepts similar to those of a computer was the analytical engine designed by Charles Babbage, a British Mathematician in 1833. The analytical engine contained many features similar to those found in today's computers. This machine could not become popular as it was very difficult to produce it. Hence the effort failed due to the non-availability of suitable technology. Unfortunately he was unable to produce a working model due to lack of precision engineering but his principles paved way to designing of other digital computers.

The **next landmark** in this direction was the effort of Herman Hollerith who first developed electromechanical calculating machines in 1890. These machines used punched card input and performed simple arithmetic calculations and card sorting operations. They were controlled by hand wired control panels.

The **first fully automated calculating machine** designed by Howard A. Aikon of Harvard University in collaboration with IBM in the year 1944 was called MARK1. It was an electronic computer, but utilised electromagnetic relays and mechanical counters. The design is based on the punched card machinery. MARK 1 was electromechanical rather than an electronic device.

The **first electronic computer** was called Atanasoff-Berry computer or ABC, after its inventor's name and his assistant, Cliford Berry. It used 45 vacuum tubes for internal logic and capacitors. The Electronic Numerical Integrator and Calculator was the first electronic computer. It was produced at Moore College of Engineering at the University of Pennsylvania, USA by a design team lead by Prof. J. Presper Eckert, and John Mauchly. The ENIAC could perform a multiplication in three thousandths of a second (1/3000 of a second). It was a huge machine with 18000 vacuum tubes and occupied a space of 10 ft. high, 10 ft. wide and some 100 ft. long.

A group of experts working at Cambridge University, England had created a machine EDSAC (Electronic Delay Storage Automatic Computer). **EDSAC was the first computer** to perform arithmetic and logical operations without human intervention, depending solely on stored instructions. The Universal Automatic Computer **(UNIVAC) was the first digital computer** built in the 1951 by J.W. Mauchly and J.P. Eckert and was commercially made available. This event marked the beginning of what is popularly known as **the first generation of computers.**

1.2.1 ABACUS

Abacus is the simplest form of a digital computer. It is interesting to note that it is still calculates at amazing speed. It looks like GINTARA. It is also interesting to note that the method of subtraction used in Abacus was based on the principle of complement of a number, a very important concept used in modern digital computer.

1.2.2 PASCAL'S CALCULATOR

For inventing the first mechanical calculating machine in 1642, the credit goes to the great French Mathematician Blaise Pascal. His machine was the first calculator in the right sense and was able to add, subtract efficiently.

In Pascal's machine, addition was straightforward and subtraction was done by the method of complement of numbers, a method used in modern computers. The machine became very popular and was produced on mass scale. Professor Nikalus Wirth at Zurich, in the year 1960 developed a programming language and named it PASCAL.

1.2.3 CHARLES BABBAGE'S DIFFERENCE ENGINE

The year 1823 could be considered a golden year in the history of Computer Science when an Englishman, Charles Babbage, a professor of mathematics of Cambridge University developed and demonstrated a working model of a mechanical computer called Difference Engine. His Engine could evaluate algebraic expressions correctly and was also able to produce mathematical and statistical tables correct up to 20 digits. For this work, *Babbage is considered to be the father of modern digital computers.*

Babbage designed Analytical Machine in 1833 which was an automatic computing machine designed to do additions at the rate of 60 per minute and had memory also. Unlike the modern computers, his Analytical Engine was to have five units viz. Store, Mill (ALU), Control, Input and Output.

1.2.4 LADY ADA LOVELACE

Babbage's life history would be incomplete without a mention of an amateur mathematician who was his disciple, namely Lady Ada Lovelace, the daughter of famous English poet Lord Byron. She developed a special number system called Binary Number System for

Babbage's Analytical Machine. *If Babbage is considered the father of modern computer science, then Lady Ada Lovelace must be thought of as first programmer in the world.*

1.2.5 ELECTRO-MECHANICAL COMPUTERS

Until the 1930's the development of automatic computing was mostly in improving the technology of calculators. The growth of computer after the end of World War II was very amazing but this *development took in five distinct phases known as computer generations.*

In fact, the scientists and engineers were more conscious about the Second World War. They started working to make computers that would help in artillery calculations and code breaking. For this purpose, the money was easily available to them, several wartime computers made their appearance. Some of them were the German ENIGMA and the British COLOSSUS, which were used by the military for code breaking. However, the *ENIAC from the USA was the first large electronic computer to become functional.*

1.2.6 ENIAC (ELECTRONIC NUMERICAL INTEGRATOR AND COMPUTER):1946

The first large scale, all value computers, called Electronic Numerical Integrator and Computer (ENIAC). It was made in 1946 by J. P. Eckert and J.W. Marchly at the University of Pennsylvania of USA. It was developed as a result of military need. It was voluminous in size and needed a space of 20ft × 40ft. The power needed by the computer was enough to light up a small township. It was a very fast machine as compared to its ancestors, which could perform 5000 additions or 350 multiplications in one second. It contained 18000 vacuum tubes, 70000 resistors, 10000 capacitors and 60000 switches. The ENIAC suffered from two shortcomings:

- It could store only a small amount of information.
- Its programs were wired on boards which made the task of modifying a program quite difficult.

However, whatever the shortcomings of ENIAC, it, represented an impressive feal of electronic engineering and was used till 1955 to solve ballistic problems, i.e. problems dealing with the weapons.

1.2.7 EDSAC (ELECTRONIC DELAYED STORAGE AUTOMATIC COMPUTER):1947-49

The wiring board seriously handicapped the operation of ENIAC. This problem was later overcome by the new concept of "Stored Program" developed by Dr. John von Neumann in 1946. He delivered a series of lectures on Electronic Digital Computers and presented a report. The basic idea behind his report was the use of binary numbers to represent data and instructions, a sequence of instructions as well as data can be stored in the memory of the computer for the purpose of automatically directing the flow of operations. The EDSAC was the first computer which used Neumann's idea of stored program. It was developed by a group of scientists headed by Prof. Wilkes at the Cambridge University.

1.2.8 EDVAC (ELECTRONIC DISCRETE VARIABLE AUTOMATIC COMPUTER):1946-52

This was another computer, which used this idea of von Neumann. It was built in 1950 at Moore School in USA. The Program and data were fed to the EDVAC through a punched paper tape. The **EDVAC** was designed on stored programs concept. The stored program concept considerably influenced the development of modern digital computers and because of this feature we often refer to modern digital computer as stored program digital computers.

1.2.9 LEO (LYONS ELECTRONIC OFFICE): 1951

M.V. Wilkes developed this first commercial computer in 1951.

1.2.10 UNIVAC I (UNIVERSAL AUTOMATIC COMPUTER): 1951

The Universal Automatic Computer (UNIVAC) was the first digital computer, which was not "one of a kind". Many UNIVAC machines were produced, the first of which was installed in the Census Bureau in 1951 and was used continuously for 10 years. It was developed by Universal Accounting Company set up by Eckert and Mauchly. It was different from its predecessors in the sense that it was a self-checking computer and used magnetic tape as input media. UNIVAC I is remembered even today for having predicted correctly the election of President Dwight Eisenhower of USA in the year 1952. Another achievement of this computer was established in the year 1954, when GEC (General Electric Corporation) used it for business application for the first time and this corporation undertook the mass scale production of the computer.

1.3 GENERATIONS

While it would not be wrong to say that the evolution of the computer began with the man's need to count, the actual growth of this field happened in a short span of thirty years. This rapid development was characterized by phases of growth, which have come to be called **computer generations.** The custom of referring to the computer era in terms of "Generations" came into wide use after 1964. Originally, the term **Generation** was used to distinguish between varying hardware technologies. But since 1968, it has been extended to include both **hardware** and **software,** which together make up a complete computer system. Other factors those are taken into consideration while differentiating one generation from another are Cost, Space, Speed & Capacity. Of course, all these factors are related both to hardware and software. In the mid-forties valves were being used as components in these machines. This was called the *First Generation* of computers. In a span of ten years, transistors that were more efficient and cheaper replaced valves. This became the *Second Generation*. In the early sixties, a major breakthrough was achieved when hundreds of transistors could be placed on a single silicon chip. This Integrated Chip (IC) became the basis of the *Third Generation.* With the introduction of VLSI (Very Large Scale Integration), thousands of transistors could be placed on a single chip. This was the *Fourth Generation* of computers. The *Fifth Generation* of computer tries to infuse intelligence into computers, also called Artificial Intelligence.

Generation	*Period*	*Characteristics*
1st Generation	1946-60	Vacuum Tubes
2nd Generation	1961-64	Transistors
3rd Generation	1965-70	Integrated Circuits (ICs)
4th Generation	1971-85	Large Scale Integrated Circuits (LSI) and Very Large Scale Integrated Circuits (VLSI)
5th Generation	1985-	Artificial Intelligence

1.3.1 FIRST GENERATION (1950s)

The computers developed during 1950s were characterised by the use of vacuum tubes were used in electronic circuits. The early computers like ENIAC, EDVAC, and EDSAC are the first generation computers. They had very small internal memories based on relays or magnetic drums. The machines were physically large and utilised punched-card-oriented slow input/output devices and low level symbolic language of programming.

1.3.2 SECOND GENERATION (LATE 1950s AND EARLY 1960s)

The second generation of computers was based on a newly invented electronic device known as the transistor. The transistor, a smaller and more reliable successor to the vacuum tube, did not require any heating element was invented in 1947.

1.3.3 THIRD GENERATION (LATE 1960s AND 1970s)

The third generation of computers emerged in the late 1960s and was developed through the 1970s. The new computers were based on solid state electronics but the novel feature was the use of *integrated circuits.* With the increasing advancements made in ;the electronic technology and the advent of "micro-electronics" technology, made it possible to integrate the large number of circuit elements into very small (less than 5 mm) surface of silicon known as "chips". This new technology was called Integrated Chips (ICs).

Important characteristics of this generation of computers include:

a. Magnetic core and solid state main storage,
b. Smaller size,

c. More flexibility, better performance and reliability,
d. Remote processing and time sharing through communication,
e. Extensive use of higher level programming language, and
f. The speed of operation of these computers was in the order of nanosecond (i.e., 1/1000,000,000th second)

Some of the mainframe computers which belong to this generation are:

IBM– 360 series
ICL – 1900 series
IBM – 370/168
ICL – 2900
Honeywell – 6000 series

1.3.4 FOURTH GENERATION (LATE 1970s AND EARLY 1980s)

The development of microprocessor made it possible to place complete control processing unit of a computer on a single chip. Magnetic core memories were replaced by semiconductor memory and microcomputers became not only interrogative but also user friendly being menu driven. Memory size increased up to 16 megabytes. In the initial period, the integrated circuits (IC) were confined to only about ten to twenty components, named as small-scale integration. With the advancements in technology it became possible to integrate hundred components on a single chip. This technology was known as *medium scale integration*, Then came the era of large- scale integration (LSI) when it was possible to integrate over 30,000 components into a single chip. Efforts are on to integrate million components on a single chip (size of a postage stamp) known as very large- scale storage integration (VLSI). The use of large scale integration (LSI) and *very large scale integration* (VLSI) techniques to produce silicon chips that contain thousand of integrated components. Other new things are:

i. Increased storage capacity and speed of operation
ii. Modular design, and
iii. The advent of microprocessor and microcomputers.

1.3.5 FIFTH GENERATION

Scientists are now at work on the fifth generation computers, which have become a reality already. They aim to bring us machines with genuine IQ, the ability to reason logically, and with real knowledge of the world. The fifth generation machines are going to be based on increasingly sophisticated electronics and artificial intelligence. These systems would have a natural language interface using Knowledge Information Processing System (KIPS) and problem solving software. In application, it will behave like an expert. The most striking features of the fifth generation computers, as put up by the Japanese Project is "The odds of coming out with fifth generation computer are heaviest and they have already started working in this direction a few years back. Japan has chosen PROLOG (Programming in Logic) language as operating software and plans to have the final machines, talk with human beings; see and deliver pictures and hear the normal and natural language."

1.4 TYPES OF COMPUTERS

Computers can basically be divided into three types:

1.4.1 Digital
1.4.2 Analog
1.4.3 Hybrid

1.4.1 DIGITAL COMPUTERS

A digital computer is a counting device. That is to say that a digital computer operates on electronic inputs (signals or pulses) that are on-off or incrementally-stepped quantities represented by numerical digits. In other words, all quantities are expressed as numbers (binary) and the computer operates on discrete numbers. Digital computers are used in data or information processing activities.

1.4.2 ANALOG COMPUTERS

An analog computer operates by measuring rather than by counting. The basic difference between the earlier type and the analog computer is simple as analog computer measures, but a digital computer counts.

1.4.3 HYBRID COMPUTERS

Hybrid computers utilise the best qualities of both the computers, and are mostly used for automatic operations of complicated physical processed and machines. But these are mostly hidden as in medical machine say ultrasound or CT scan.

1.5 GENERAL CHARACTERISTICS

The fact that computers have made their impact on almost all aspects of life in today's world can hardly be questioned. The question that you may ask here is how you benefit from using a computer. A computer provides five basic benefits:

- Speed
- Accuracy
- Diligence
- Versatility
- Power remembrance

Computers work at very high speed and are much faster than humans. The human equivalent of an average computer would be one million mathematicians working 24 hours a day. Computers rarely make mistakes. In fact, most computer errors are caused by human frailties. Unlike humans, computers simply do not get bored or tired. The monotony of repetitive work does not affect computers.

However, computers cannot take over all activities simply because they are less flexible than humans are. They have to be explicitly told what to do; they cannot perform anything outside the defined scope. If an unanticipated situation arises, computers will either produce erroneous results or abandon the task altogether. They do not have the potential to work out an alternative solution.

REFERENCES

1. Barness, J, Susan– Becoming a Digital Library, New York: Marcel Decker, 2002.
2. David, Bawden – Understanding Digital Library Towards a Conceptual Framework, Boston: British Library Research Innovation Centre, 2002.
3. Dokter, F – Digital Electronics, London, MacMillan, 2001.
4. Dubey, Yogendra, P – Computer and Telecommunications Technology: A State of the Art, *In* Sharma and Ojha ed. - Advances in Library and Information Science, Jaipur: RBSA, 1988.
5. Emery, G – Elements of Computer Science, New Delhi: BPB, 1991.
6. German, GE., ed. – Digital Factor in Library and Information Service, London: Facct, 2002.
7. IGNOU – BLS Course Reading booklets, New Delhi, 2004.
8. NIIT – Computer Overview and DOS, New Delhi: NIIT, 1997.
9. Pace, Andrew, K – The Ultimate Digital Library, Chicago: American Library Association, 2000.
10. Satyanarayan, NR – Manual of Library Automation and Networking, Lucknow: Royal Book Agency, 2004.
11. Vashishth, CP ed. – Computerisation and Library Network, New Delhi: ILA, 1991.
12. Webb, Terry, D – Professional Issues at Library Automation, London: Hawerth Press, 2000.
13. Wills and Miller – Computers for Everybody, New Delhi: BPB, 1990.
14. Websites: infolibrarian.com, informindia.co.in, libraryworld.net, info.com/librarySoftware, library.geac.com, librarysoftwares.net , web.inflibnet.ac.in, mcitconsortium.nic.in, oclc.com, multiplayergames.in

CHAPTER 2

FUNDAMENTALS OF COMPUTER

The discovery of numbers may be considered as the greatest achievement of mankind. It led to the development of all kinds of calculating devices. Today, it is impossible to imagine a world without numbers. The discovery of zero by Indian mathematicians laid the foundation of number system. Now, we will see how man has reached the computer age from the Stone Age.

Necessity is the mother of invention. This saying holds true for computers also because computers were invented as a result of man's search for a fast and accurate calculating device. It is believed that the Abacus was the first calculating device, which was invented in China in 3000 BC. From Abacus to the macro computer, the counting systems have undergone a tremendous change. The efforts are still continuing to make the computer more and more versatile.

2.1 CLASSIFICATION AND CATEGORIES

Parameters for Classification

- Performance,
- Measures in terms of Speed, Data storage, Capacity, Ability to handle a large number of Input & Output devices and nature of Operations it can perform (simple word processing to complex scientific calculations),
- Size.
- Cost.

Categories of Computer Systems

2.1.1 Microcomputers (also referred as Micro's)
2.1.2 Minicomputers (also referred as Mini's)

2.1.3 Mainframe computers
2.1.4 Supercomputers

2.1.1 MICRO COMPUTERS

Micro computer is called Micro for two reasons: one, because it is miniature in size (micro means million times less than a unit quantity) and secondly because it uses micro processors. Micro processor is actually the heart-cum-mind of a computer. Microcomputers are the lowest end of the computer range. They are highly visible PCs you see on desktops fall into this category.

Main features are –

- Single user systems
- Small to medium data
- Storage capacities (500 MB-2 GB)
- Processing power is limited

Applications— These systems are used for:

- Word processing
- Spreadsheet calculation
- Database management
- Desktop publishing
- Accounting & statistical analysis
- Graphics designing
- Investment analysis
- Project management; and
- Teaching & entertainment

  e.g. IBM PC, PS/2 & Apple Macintosh

The microcomputers are further subdivided into two categories:

i. Personal Computer
ii. Home Computer

The Personal Computer

The most popular form of the computer in use today is probably the Personal Computer (PC). The PC can be used for various applications and, in fact, there are millions of PCs already in use by individuals and organizations. The PC is small in size but capable enough to handle large tasks. It can perform a diverse range of functions, from keeping track of household accounts to keeping records of the stores of a large manufacturing company.

Speed	100 Kips (kilo instruction per second)
Word length	8 to 32 bits
Storage capacity	640 KB to 80 GB
Areas of applications	• Engineering and scientific application • Accounting & financial analysis • Word processing • Computer graphics
Cost	Rs. 10,000 to less than 1,00,000

2.1.2 MINICOMPUTERS

Minicomputers perform better, are larger in size and cost more than micros. They are designed for –

- Multi user systems
- Larger storage capacities
- Higher speed operations
- Faster peripheral devices like high speed printers
- Communicate with mainframes

Applications

- Used for data processing for a medium sized organization
- Used for control & monitor production, processes, analyze results of experiments in laboratories etc.
- Used as server in Local Area Networks (LAN)

Speed	500 Mips (Meta instruction per second)
Word length	16 bits
Storage capacity	256 KB - 1 MB
Areas of applications	• Engineering and scientific application • Process control in industry • Time showing service
Cost	Rs. 1,00,000 – 5,00,000

e.g. Digital Equipment's PDP 11/45 and VAX 11

2.1.3 MAINFRAME COMPUTERS

Mainframes are more powerful than Minis. They operate at very high speeds, have very large storage capacities and can support hundreds of users. They are used in large organizations for large-scale jobs.

Speed	10 Mips (Meta instruction per second)
Word length	32-48 bits
Storage capacity	2 MB-16 MB
Areas of applications	• Engineering designs, scientific research • Large scale reservation systems • On line communication
Cost	Rs. 50,00,000

Applications

1. Used for data processing in large organizations
2. Used to manage large centralized databases
3. Used as controlling nodes in Wide Area Networks (WAN)
   e.g. IBM 3000, UNIVAC 1180

2.1.4 SUPERCOMPUTERS

Supercomputers are at the apex of the computer range. They are the fastest and the most expensive machines, and are considered a national resource. There are less than 500 conventional supercomputers in the world.

Speed	100 Mips (Meta instruction per second)
Word length	64-96 bits
Storage capacity	8MB to 64 MB
Areas of applications	• Weather prediction
	• Crystallographic analysis • Design of complicated machines i.e. Supersonic jets, space research

Applications

- Used for complex scientific and defense applications.
- Used for weather forecasting, bio-medical research and aircraft design.

2.2 INPUT AND OUTPUT DEVICES

2.2.1 MOUSE

A mouse is an input device that is used to point and select an option on the VDU.

Types of Mouse: A mouse can be classified on the basis of the number of buttons on it, has the technology it uses and the kind of interface it has with the computer. A mouse may have one, two or three buttons.

Mechanical Mouse

In a mechanical mouse, the ball that projects through the button surface rotates as the mouse is moved along a flat surface. The direction on rotation is detected and relayed to the computer by the switches inside the mouse.

Optical Mouse

An optical mouse uses a light beam instead of a rotating ball to detect movement across a specially patterned mouse pad.

2.2.2 SCANNERS

Another INPUT device that is being increasingly used is the scanner. Scanners are used to reproduce photographs.

Types of Scanners

Flatbed Scanner

It works like a photocopier. It can scan and store images from books without having to remove the page, which is difficult in the case if the roller feed scanner.

Roller-Feed Scanner

In a roller-feed scanner, the image is passed over a roller where it is captured.

2.2.3 TOUCH SCREENS

A touch screen Input interface are normally used when information has to be accessed with minimum effort.

Two popular technologies exist for tough screens. In one, the screen is made sensitive to touch and the exact position is detected. In the other, the screen is lined with light emitting devices and photo-detectors. When the user's finger approaches the screen, the light beam is broken and is detected by the photo-detectors.

Generally used by travel agents, airline and railway reservation counters, and also used in stock exchanges.

2.2.4 LIGHT PENS

A light pen is a pointing device that can be used to select an option by simply painting at it or drawing figures directly on the screen.

A light pen has a photo detector at its tips. Light pens are useful for menu based applications. Instead of moving the mouse around or using a keyboard, the user can select an option by pointing at it. A light pen is also useful for drawing graphics in CAD (Computer Aided Design).

2.2.5 PRINTERS

* Details available at Hardware part at 2.5.2

2.2.6 PLOTTERS

A plotter is an Output device that is used to create presentation Visuals, Charts, Graphs, Tables and diagrams.

Types of Plotters

Flatbed Plotter

In flatbed plotters, the paper is held stationary while the arm and pens move over it.

Drum Plotter

In drum plotter, the paper is wrapped around a drum and anchored at both ends. The drum rotates while pen moves laterally along a fixed rail.

To draw clear, high quality diagrams, a plotter needs high quality pens with special inks of different colours. A plotter can be connected to a PC through the parallel port.

Plotters are used in applications like CAD (Computer Aided Design) which requires high quality graphics on paper.

2.3 STORAGE MEDIA

User needs to be stored for later use on storage media. If the data that needs to be stored is small, floppy disks are enough.

2.3.1 FLOPPY DISKS

* Full Detail in Memory Part at 2.5.3

However, when the amount of date to be stored is huge, storage media with large storage capacity are required. Such storage media are-

- Cartridge Tape
- CD-ROM
- Magneto-Optical Disks

2.3.2 CARTRIDGE TAPE

A cartridge tape is a very convenient backup media as it can store many megabytes of data. Cartridge tapes are available in capacities of 60 MB, 150 MB and 500 MB.

A cartridge tape is made of plastic, coated with a magnetic material and is similar to a video cassette tape. Data on a cartridge tape is stored sequentially. Cartridge tape drives are present only in large machines.

2.3.3 CD-ROM

The CDs used in a CD-ROM are similar to audio CDs and can store vast quantity of data 600 MB or more. To read a CD-ROM, you need an input device called the CD-ROM drive. A CD-ROM can not be erased or written onto without the help of a special device called the CD-Recorder.

CD-ROMs are used whenever large volumes of data need to be stored and distributed. Databases on medicine, tourism, literatim on Science & Technology etc. are available on CD-ROMs. Encyclopedia and Dictionaries are also available on CD-ROMs.

2.3.4 MAGNETO-OPTICAL DISK

Maxell Corporation, USA has developed a 3.5 inch Magneto-Optical (M-O) disk, having storage capacities in access of 640 MB. M-O disks with capacities of 2 GB are also available. Data can be read as well as written onto these disks. The new disk is compatible with all 3.5" M-O drives such as those manufactured by Fujitsu, Olympus, and others.

Some of the significant improvements of the M-O Disk over the conventional 1.44 MB diskette are:

- Write speed that is more than 100% faster than the conventional media.
- If the M-O disk is double sided, it can store up to 4 GB of data, which is more than that many hard disks can store.
- An archival life of more than 30 years, the disks are re-writable over 1 million times.
- Protective layer if exceptionally durable hard coating to safeguard surface from heat or moisture.

Applications

Mass archival storage, document/image storage, and multimedia storage using data impression technology.

2.4 CLASSIFICATION OF PERSONAL COMPUTERS

Computers falling under the class of PCs can be classified into 2 broad groups:

2.4.1 Desktops
2.4.2 Portables

2.4.1 Desktops: Desktops cannot be carried around and used while you are traveling e.g. IBM PS/2 systems & Apples' Macintosh range of Computer.

2.4.2 Portables: There are essentially three classes of portables:

1. Laptops
2. Notebooks
3. Palmtop

Class	*Size*	*Weight*	*Power*	*Examples*
Laptops	Small, slim attach case	7 -12 kg.	Same power as a desktop PC	Toshiba 5200 (from Toshiba) from SLT/286 (from Compaq)
Notebooks	Size of a notebook (21 x 29.5cm. approx.)	3 - 4 kg.	Same power as a desktop PC	Contura 3/20 (from Compaq) Acer Anjware (from Zenith Computers Ltd.)
Palmtops	Size of a pocket calculator	Varies	Not the same power of desktop PC	Hewlett Packard's HP95 LX comes configured with Lotus 1-2-3

Block Diagram of Computer

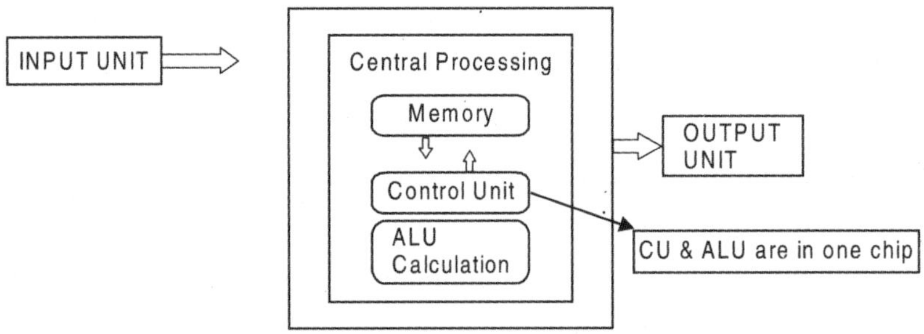

[Whenever we require giving instruction to computer to perform any work, control unit part of CPU activates the input device (e.g. Key Board, Mouse, Joystick and Light Pen) to bring information into memory. This information/instruction then goes to ALU with the help of Control Unit. In ALU all the mathematical work completed and then results again transferred to the memory. Finally result can be obtained as output device (e.g. Monitor, Printer and Secondary memory).]

2.5 COMPUTER WORKING SYSTEMS

Working parts of Hardware and Software

Working Parts of Hardware and Software

Hardware (Computer Machine Parts)	*Software (Computer Programs i.e., INSTRUCTION)*
• CVT – Constant Voltage Transformer UPS – Un-interrupted Power Supply	• Application Software – for individual requirement e.g. CLMS
• CPU – Central Processing Unit	• Utility Software - for general requirement
• VDU – Visual Display Unit	– Spread Sheet e.g. Lotus 1-2-3
• MOUSE	– Graphics e.g. Lotus 1-2-3
• KEY BOARD	– Word Processing e.g. WS4
• PRINTER	• System Software (Operating System) – Single User e.g. DOS – Multi-user e.g. UNIX, LAN, WAN

Print Media & Electronic Media

Method	*Medium*	*Output Device*
Printed	Hard copy	• Printer • Character printers • Matrix • Daisy wheel • Thermal • Ink jacket • Line printers • Barrel • Chain • Page printer • Laser printer
Image Recording: Computer Output on Microfilm	*Microfilm or Microfiche*	*COM Reader Microfilm*
Visual	Screen play	Visual Display Unit (Work Station or terminal)
Graphical	Charts, graphs, diagrams	Graph plotter Printer plotter
Magnetic used also as input and storage media because of its multi use features	Floppy disk Exchangeable disk storage (EDS) Winchester disk High capacity fixed disks Data module	

Components of Personal Computer

2.5.1 HARDWARE

All the equipment or parts of Computer Machine, which one can touch, feel and see are called Hardware e.g. VDU, CPU etc.

CVT

It is Constant Voltage Transformer, which controls voltage.

Current – 220 V   Volt - 0.5 kV = 500 Volt

UPS

It gives Constant Voltage and backup both.

CPU

Whenever we require giving instruction to computer to perform any work, control unit part of Central Processing Unit (CPU) activates the input device (e.g. Key Board, Mouse, Joystick and Light Pen) to bring information into memory. This information/instruction then goes to ALU with the help of Control Unit. In ALU all the mathematical work completed and then results again transferred to the memory. Finally result can be obtained as output device (e.g. Monitor, Printer and Secondary memory).

Key Board

* Beginning stage : 93-97 Keys
* Middle stage : 101 Keys (Standard)
* Present stage : 105 Keys (Standard with 2 win Key, 1 right menu Key turbo key)
  *Turbo Plus KB – for Home & Office (105 Keys)

Information at Back Side

(PC AT/XT – 101 Keys)

PC–Personal Computer
AT–Advanced Technology
XT–Extended Technology

Key Board (Front Side)

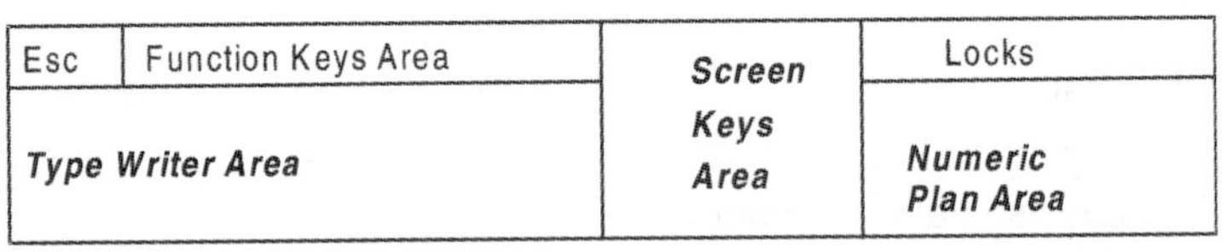

VDU (VISUAL DISPLAY UNIT/MONITOR)

Monitor is an output device. It is also known as VDU. Monitor is in the form of TV Screen without sound system except some cases. It consists of a **Cathode Ray Tube** (CRT), in which electrons are emitted by cathode by heating of filament by electron gun. These emitted electrons are fallen over florescent screen to convert it into a picture. In VDU roster screen help to convert beam of electrons produced by electron gun into a picture. It scans the screen back and forth from left hand corner to bottom right hand corner in a very high speed and a picture are re-drawing in a very high speed, which we can not distinguish. Many small cells constitute the screen of monitor. These cells are known as Pixels in a given area known as resolution.

---

* Small points – Florescent point (bright with electric) called Pixels.
* Points scroll left to right draw 60 times in a second.
* Human eyes differentiate only 16 times draw scroll.

Types of Monitors –

- Monochrome (Black/White)
- LCD (Liquid Crystal Display) - Monitors are best for use.
- Colour Monitor (Color 16 or 256)

2.5.2 PRINTERS

It is an output device and they are of 2 types –

- Impact Printer - through carbon ribbon i.e. Dot Matrix
- Non Impact - without ribbon i.e. Laser

Impact Printers

These are those printers in which characters are printed on to the paper through the impact on carbon ribbon that means characters are printed on paper against the carbon ribbon.

Types Impact Printer – 1. Character
2. Line
3. Page

Character Printer

These are those printers in which a character is printed at a time. Types of these Printers are as follows:

Dot Matrix printer

In this type of printer, characters are printed in the form of dots. The speed of this printer is 40-250 character/second but the printing quality of this printer is very bad and it is also very noisy.

Daisy wheel printer

It works in a same manner to golf ball typewriter but the speed of this printer is lesser than the Dot Matrix printer. Printing quality is slightly better than the Dot Matrix printer and also less noisy.

Thimble printer

In this printer, characters are in the shape of thimble and characters are around the edge (text). Thimble printer works like a daisy wheel printer.

Spark printer

Spark printer is also called as electrostatic printer. This printer has aluminum-coded sheet in which electric sparks turns the character on to the paper.

Line Printer

These printers print one line at a time. Some examples are Drum Printer & Chain Printer.

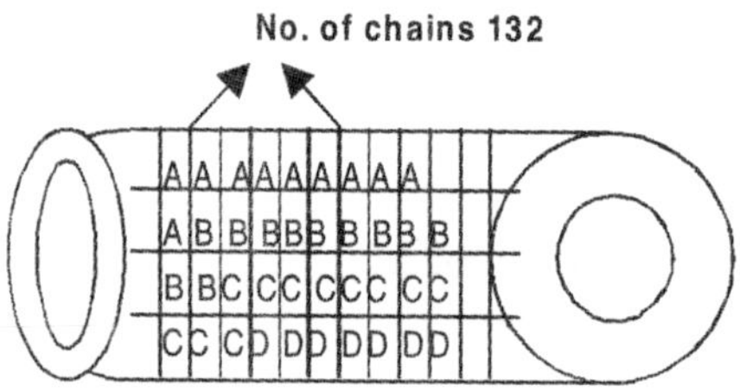

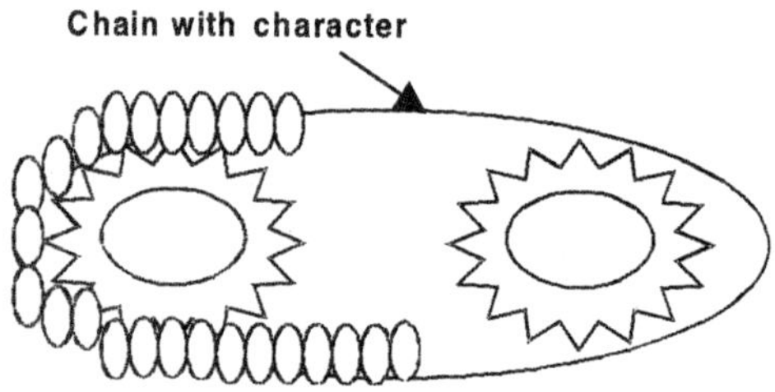

Page Printer

These are those printers, which print a page at a time. E.g. Laser Printer

> *LASER PRINTER-* Prints with the help of laser rays. The speed of this printer is 14 pages per minute. The character style of this printer is also in the form of dots but the size of dots is so small that we cannot see them at the time of printing. These are two types i.e. Ink Jet and Desk Jet.

Non-Impact Printer

These are those in which we can directly print character by heating on to the paper.
They are of two types –

1. Graph plotter
2. Inkjet printer.

Graph Plotter

It is electromechanical device with a moving arm which itself moves along a sheet of paper. It uses signals from computer to draw a graph.

Inkjet Printer

It fires ink drop on to the paper by using a electrostatic field. Its printer head has a nozzle which fires a jet electrically charged ink on the paper to form characters.

2.5.3 MEMORY

Memory of computer classified as below:

Primary	*Secondary (In/Out Side Computer)*
• RAM - Random Access Memory • ROM - Read Only Memory – ROM – PROM – EROM – EEROM	• Punch Card • Magnetic Tape • Floppy Disc • Hard Disc • Compact Disc (CD)

Primary Memory

It is also called as semi-conductor memory. The memory which exist inside to the computer known as primary memory. This is of 2 types:

RAM (Random Access Memory)

It is a volatile memory. In RAM the data can be saved, till the power supply to the computer. As we cut off the power of computer, data saved in computer washes away. In this type of memory read and write process can be done randomly i.e. at any location of the memory.

ROM (Read Only Memory)

It is a non-volatile memory. In this type of memory the saved data cannot be destroyed due to power cut. In this type of memory read & write operations can also be done randomly i.e. at any memory location. ROM are of following types:

- ROM – Read Only Memory
- PROM – Programmable Read Only Memory
- EPROM – Erasable Programmable Read Only Memory
- EEPROM – Electrically Erasable Programmable Read Only Memory

In ROM all data is already feeded by manufacturer at the time of computer assembling. There is no place for feeding other data or instruction but this facility is provided in PROM. There was some extra space for programming. PROM has a disadvantage that once we write any data or instruction in PROM we can't erase them. In EE-PROM, manufacturer provides this erasing facility of data. For this ultraviolet rays were used. Thereafter instead of ultraviolet rays electrical signals are using to erase data from memory. This type of memory is known as EE-ROM.

Secondary Memory

A memory, which can exist outside to the computer, is known as secondary memory. These are of following types:

i. Punch Card
ii. Magnetic Tape
iii. Floppy Disk
iv. Compact Disc
v. Magnetic Hard Disk

Punch Card

A punch card is a piece of stiff paper that contains digital information represented by the presence or absence of holes in predefined positions. Almost an obsolete recording medium, punched cards were widely used throughout the nineteenth century for controlling textile looms and through the twentieth century in unit record machines for input, processing, and data storage. Early digital computers used punched cards as the primary medium for input of both computer programmes and data, with offline data entry on key punch machines.
Punch cards were first used around 1725 by Basile Bouchon and Jean Baptiste Falcon as a more robust form of the perforated paper rolls then in use for controlling textile looms in France. This technique was greatly improved by Joseph Marie Jacquard in his Jacquard loom in 1801. A few decades later Charles Babbage launched the idea of the use of the punched cards as a way to control a mechanical calculator he designed. Herman Hollerith developed punched card data processing technology for the 1890 US Census and founded the *Tabulating Machine Company* (1896) which was one of three companies that merged to form Computing Tabulating Recording Corporation (CTR), later renamed IBM. IBM manufactured and marketed a variety of unit record machines for creating, sorting, and tabulating punched cards, even after expanding into computers in the late 1950s. IBM developed punch card technology into a powerful tool for business data-processing and produced an extensive line of general purpose unit record machines. By 1950, the IBM card and IBM unit record machines had become ubiquitous in industry and government.

Few Punch cards are: Hollerith's punch card, UNIVAC 90-character punch card and IBM Port-A-Punch.

Magnetic Tape

Magnetic tape memory is similar to commonly used audio tape recorders. The data recorded on a tape can be retrieved sequentially in the order in which they are written. Thus if a desired record is at the end of a tape that all the earlier records have to be read before it is reached. The accusative of magnetic tape is very high compared to that stored on a disc. The tapes are primarily used to save old information for long periods of time.

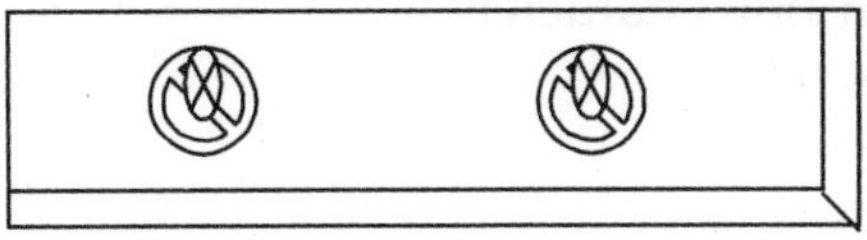

Floppy Disk

It is a small secondary storage device, which can be used for both input and output operations. Floppy discs are made of magnetic oxide coated Mauler computer tape material. The flexible tape material is cut into circular pieces of 5+1/4" or 3+1/2" in diameter. As the material used is not a hard plate but a flexible tape, so it is called as Floppy disc. According to size, floppy disc are of following types- As per Jacket size (in inches)

i. Standard Size – 8"
ii. Mini Floppy – $5^{1/4"}$ - Lower density (360 KB) - High density (1.2 MB)
iii. Micro Floppy- $3^{1/2"}$ - Lower density (720 KB) - High density (1.44 MB)

Storage capacity of floppy is small compared to other storage devices but retrieval of information is very quick.

Parts of Floppy

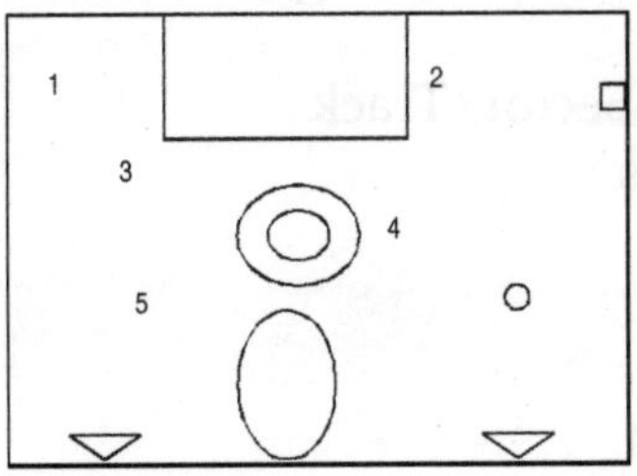

1. External Volume Label
2. Write protect Notch
3. Disc Drive Hub
4. Index hole
5. Access Window

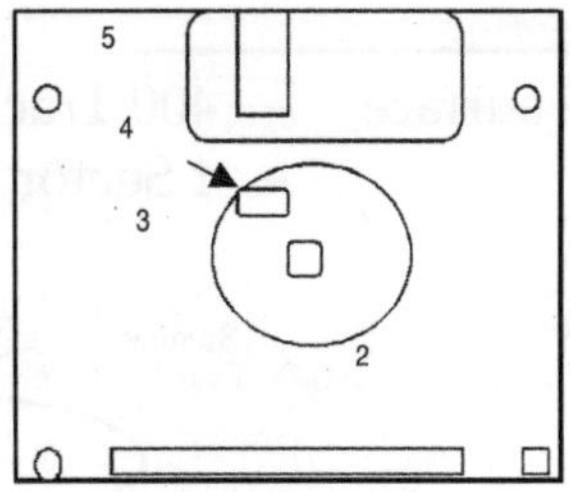

Floppy (1.2 MB)

Floppy (1.44MB)

POINTS TO REMEMBER

* One side of Low density floppy has 40 Track and 9 Sector
* One side (40*9) = 180 KB
  So both side = 360 KB

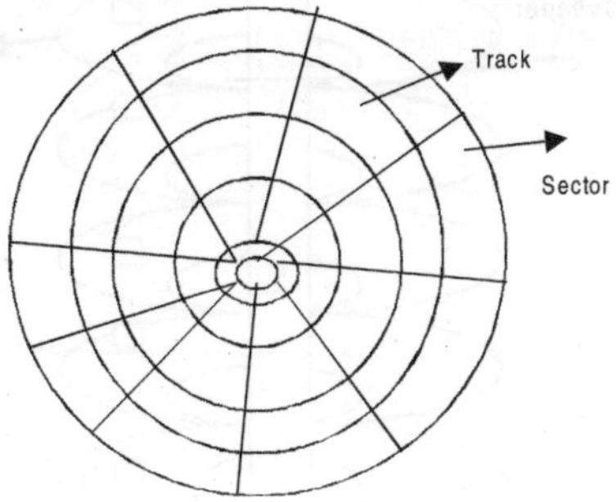

Compact Disk

Computer Data Unit is Byte

Computer takes 8 bits in one character, which is equal to 1 Bytes.

Storage Capacity:

1 Sector	=	512 Bytes
1024 Bytes	=	1KB (Kilo Bytes)
10^6 Bytes	=	1MB (Mega Bytes)
10^{12} Bytes	=	1GB (Giga Bytes)

Hard Disk

Magnetic hard disks are used as input/ output device and for computer auxiliary memory. A magnetic disk is similar to gramophone record but is coated with Ferro magnetic materials and rotates with a very high speed of 1800 rotation per minute to 3600 rpm. In a magnetic disk we can have direct access of any information from any location irrespective of its location on disk. Magnetic disk as similar to floppy disk plates on a spindle. Smooth metal plates coated with Ferro magnetic substances on both sides are fixed on spindle, there may be 6 plates or more than 6, depends upon capacity of hard disk. These plates one below another make up a disk pack. A disk pack is mounted over a disk driver. A disk driver has also a set of magnetic heads mounted on arms. Information are stored on the surface of disk, top most and bottom most surfaces are not used for storing the information.

For one surface	–	400 Track/Surface & 50 Sector/Track
	–	1 Sector stored 512 Bytes

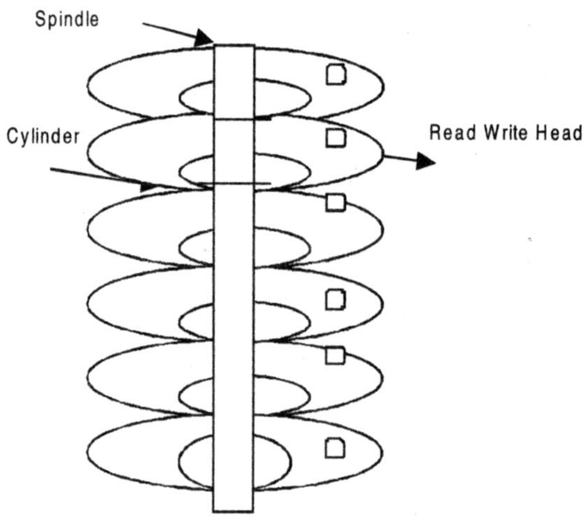

Hard Disc

2.5.4 SOFTWARE

These are programs, which are set of instructions or collection of instructions. These are of 3 types-

Application Software

This software's developed according to the need of individuals e.g. CLMS.

Utility Software

These are those programs, which are developed to meet general requirement. These are of following types:

a.	Word Processors	–	WS, & Professional Writer
b.	DBMS	–	Dbase III+, FoxPro
c.	Spread Sheet	–	MS Excel
d.	Graphics	–	Lotus 1-2-3

System Software (Operating System)

It is an interpreting program, which acts as an interpreter between men and machines. These are of two types – Single user and Multi-user Operating System. In single user system only one person can interact with machine at a time but in multi-user system more than one person can interact at a time.

e.g. Single user – MS DOS & Multi-user –UNIX.

2.5.5 LANGUAGES UNDER GENERATIONS OF COMPUTERS

i. First Generation Languages -In the beginning, the computer machine level languages are used. In this language 0 & 1 are used to give instructions to computer.

ii. Second Generation Languages - Same English terms like ADD, Sub, Multiply, Division are used along with 0 & 1. This type of language is known as **assembly language** to convert assembly language into machine level language "A" translating program is used which is known as **assembler**. The common English term which are used in assembly language known as Mnemonics. These two generation languages are commonly known as *low level language*.

iii. Third Generation Languages- All English terms are as it is used to give instruction to computer to convert this language into machine level language to translating programs are used. One of them is known as **interpreter** and another one is **compiler**. These are also programs, which convert machine level language. Some examples of these generation languages are PL-I, PASCAL, COBOL, and FORTRAN, BASIC, C. Basic difference between Interpreter and Compiler are:

Interpreter	*Compiler*
• One by one line wise conversion	• Full convert
• Faster in time	• Shorter in time
• Direct convert	• Make code file – object file in machine level language
• Error show line wise	• Full error at the end

iv. Fourth Generation Languages- Same packages are introduced such as dBase III+, Lotus 1-2-3, C+.

All application software packages are written in computer language. There are various computer languages like C, C++, FORTRAN and Pascal. Each language is best suited for a particular application. C and C++ languages are used to develop highly complex software. FORTRAN is used for scientific applications. Each language has its own vocabulary. There are some packages like FoxPro, MS Access and Sybase that are more English-like. Thus, even non-computer professionals, i.e. executives and managers who have never studied computer science, can learn to use these languages.

2.5.6 HIGH-LEVEL LANGUAGES

The following are the high-level languages that are currently in widespread use:

- **ALGOL** (Algorithmic Language) A language developed for mathematical and scientific purposes.
- **APL** (A Programming Language) A powerful language for interactive computing.
- **BASIC** (Beginners All-purpose Symbolic Instruction Code) an easily learned language especially poplar on microcomputers.
- **COBOL** (Common Business Oriented Language) as its name implies a standardized language widely used on commercial applications.
- **FORTRAN** (Formula Translator) developed for mathematical and scientific purposes.
- **PASCAL** (named after Blaze Pascal) a block-structured language which allows user defined data types.
- **PL/1** (Programming Language/one) developed to provide the facilities of COBOL and FORTRAN in one language.
- **SQL** (Strutted Query Language) DEVELOPED by IBM to access database very efficiently. SQL is now a standard feature or every major database such as ORACLE & MS SQL.

2.5.7 DATA ORGANIZATION

In our day-to-day lives, we store information in the form of files, be it our telephone directory, or the record of monthly expenditure. The medium that is used in this type of manual storage is usually paper or other media.

Similarly, information is also stored on the computer in the form of files, but the media is either external storage or internal storage. A computer may have the following types of files on its storage media:

1. Text File

Sir,

This is to bring to your kind information...

2. Data File

Code	City
0522	LKO
0011	ND
0512	ALLD
0413	GKP

3. Graphic Files

Types of Files

Sequential File

In this type of file records are in sequence. To access the records, previous records should be scanned. In this sequential file records are added only at the end of the file. It is impossible to insert a record in the middle of the file without re-writing the file. If a user wants to access 10th record then it is necessary that first it reads all the previous 9 records then it can reach to 10th record. E.g.-Read records comes before also i.e. 1,2,3,4 if want 4.

Direct Access File (Random File)

In direct access file records are placed randomly through out the file and they are not in sequence because they are updated directly and re-written at the same location. Records are added at the end of the file or at any location. For example - read only particular record i.e. 4 only.

Index File

These are made through System.

Dynamic File

It has dual nature of sequential file and random access file. According to nature of file dynamic files are of following types:

---

i. **Master file:** It has a permanent nature.

ii. **Transition file:** It has a temporary nature.

iii. **Sort file:** When any sequential file has been kept in a particular order known as sort file.

iv. **Report file:** When data is collected from different files to give meaningful information known as report file.

2.5.8 ALGORITHM

Rough search of any task is called Algorithm.

Step 1.

```
START
INPUT A
INPUT B
C=A+B
PRINT C
STOP
```

2.5.9 FLOW CHART

Pictorial representation of Algorithm is called Flow Chart.

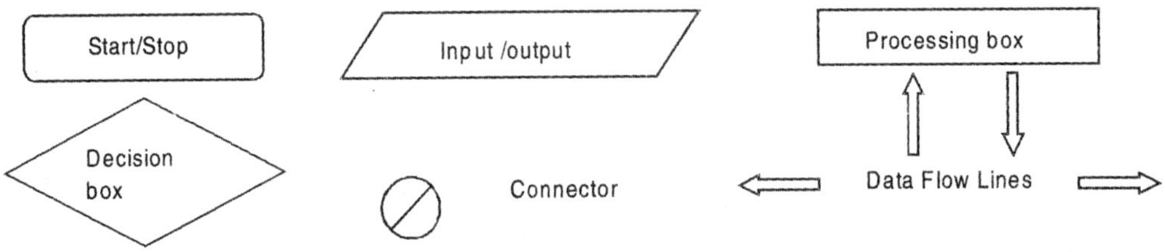

An example of Flow Chart

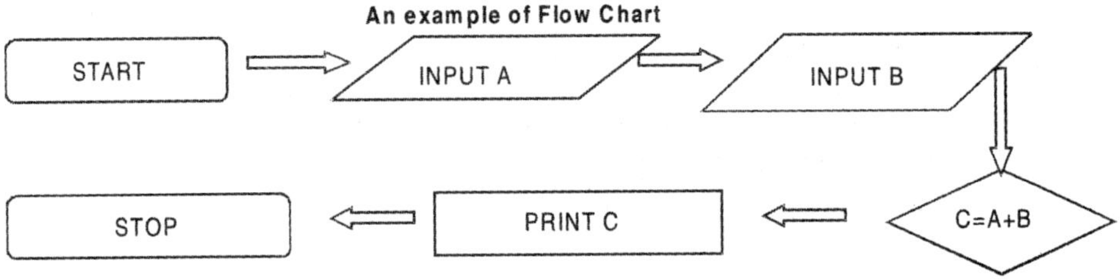

Points to Remember

- Collection of DATA item (character) is RECORD
- Collection of RECORD is DATABASE
- Collection of DATABASE is FILE
- Collection of FILE is DIRECTORY.

Keys of Key Board

Key	*Function*
Esc	Depends on the application. Usually used to cancel a command
F1-F12 (Function Keys)	Used to perform special functions that depend on the software being used.

Contd...

Enter or Return	Used to execute an instruction or data being keyed in through the keyboard
Caps lock	Used for keying in capitalized alphabets
Shift	Caps lock off : a capitalized alphabet is inputCaps lock on: reverses the above effect.
Ctrl, Alt	Pressed with other keys they input special messages to the computer
Win key	Used to return screen on windows position
Backspace	Used to erase the character to the left of the cursor position
Print Screen/SysRq	Used to print whatever is displayed on the screen/System Required; depends on the application
Scroll Lock	Used to stop the scrolling the screen, depends on application
Pause Break	Used to Break running information
Insert	Used to insert characters at the current cursor position
Del	Used to delete characters at the current cursor position
Home, End, PgUp, PgDn	Used to perform special functions viz. Beginning & End of line, Scroll Page up & Page down
Arrow Keys	Move cursor UP, DOWN, LEFT, RIGHT side
Num Lock	Used to activate the numeric keys on the Numeric keypad.

REFERENCES

1. David, Bawden – Understanding Digital Library Towards a Conceptual Framework, Boston: British Library Research Innovation Centre, 2002.
2. Dokter, F – Digital Electronics, London, MacMilan, 2001.
3. Dewey, Partick, R – CD-ROMs to Use in Your Library: Description, Evaluation and Practical Advice, New York: American Library Association, 1996.
4. Emery, G – Elements of Computer Science, New Delhi: BPB, 1991.
5. IGNOU – BLS Course Reading booklets, New Delhi, 2004.
6. Lasselle and Ramsay – ABC's of IBM PC and Compatibles, New Delhi: BPB, 1990.
7. NIIT – Computer Overview and DOS, New Delhi: NIIT, 1997.
8. Pace, Andrew, K – The Ultimate Digital Library, Chicago: American Library Association, 2000.
9. Peterson; Ann and Nancy, A, ed. Digital Library Use, London: MIT Press, 2003.
10. Robbins, J – Hard Disk Instant Reference, New Delhi: BPB, 1990.
11. Rorving, ME – Microcomputers and Libraries, New York: Knowledge Industry, 1984.
12. Satyanarayan, NR – Manual of Library Automation and Networking, Lucknow: Royal Book Agency, 2004.
13. Tripathi, SM – Documentation and Information Services and Networks, Vol. 2. Information Systems and Networks, Agra: Y.K. Publishers, 1997.
14. Webb, Terry, D – Professional Issues at Library Automation, London: Hawerth Press, 2000.
15. Websites: infolibrarian.com, informindia.co.in, libraryworld.net, info.com/librarySoftware, library.geac.com, librarysoftwares.net, web.inflibnet.ac.in, mcitconsortium.nic.in, oclc.com, multiplayergames.in

CHAPTER 3

COMPUTER SYSTEM AND AUTOMATION

The computer has become an indispensable necessity in contemporary society. Business corporation, government agencies and other organization make use of computers in a variety of activities such as data processing and management of information system.

For the last decade or so, computers are being used in India in airline operations, railways, banking sector and other fields. The library and information profession has also become aware of the potential of computer as a powerful tool, which can be utilized to improve both the operational efficiency of the library and information personnel and the quality and range of services provided to the user community. Such awareness has been reinforced by the successful experiments carried out in this direction in many of the developed countries. It is common phenomenon to see computers being used in all library and information activities in countries like UK and USA.

The availability of computing power at comparatively cheaper costs has further contributed to the present use of computers in Indian library and information profession. In other words, there is a lot of effort directed towards using computers in a big way for library and information service in India and abroad.

3.1 COMPUTER SYSTEM

A working knowledge of the components of the computer system is all that is needed to utilize a computer to solve scientific or research problems, to perform record keeping activities or to process any data. A computer system can be viewed as high-speed automatic information transformation devices (called hardware and computer program called software).

Hardware refers to the physical components of a computer, while **software** refers to a set of instructions for the computer (hardware) to follow. Computer can function only when hardware and software are combined in an appropriate manner that is both musts to compatible.

3.2 MERITS OF SOFTWARE PACKAGES

- They are economical because the investment cost for the initial creation and later maintenance of the package is spread over several users.
- The package comes as a well-tested set of programs, and the supplier has a sufficient number of clients to justify adequate maintenance arrangements.
- The software producer is likely to be a specialist in that kind of software and should therefore produce a better quality product with valuable features whose importance might not occur to the new user.
- Packages are well documented, including detailed system specification, identification of hardware requirements, input, output and file specifications and system timing, and user manuals.
- Packages are available at short notice and the system can therefore be implemented earlier.
- Support and advice services should be available from the package supplier.

3.3 LIMITATIONS OF SOFTWARE PACKAGES

- The package will probably not fit the user's present system or requirements. Its acceptability depends on how easily the package can be modified in order that a satisfactory compromise can be achieved.
- The user depends on the expertise and reliability of the software supplier, for both the initial package and subsequent maintenance and support.
- The package program is likely to be less efficient than a tailor made package in terms of computer running time and core store utilization.

3.4 UTILITY SOFTWARE

There are different kinds of software packages. Software can be broadly divided into utility software and application software.

Utility software is made available by computer equipment manufactures or software houses in order that certain basic functions may be performed; these programs include:

Sorting – assembles records into sequence
Merging – merges two files

File copying	–	copy a file held on one medium to another
File handling	–	shows file in alphabetical or other orders, renames files, displays files
Dumping routines	–	for storing data during a long processing run, to ensure that data is not lost during a breakdown
Editing routines	–	for converting output data to the format required for visual or printed output
Diagnostic or debugging routines and file recovery		
Antivirus software	–	detects viruses and disinfects discs

Different sets of utilities will support different forms or ranges of options for the above operations. For example, simple editing packages are likely to contain commands to *insert, delete, print and replace specific lines of text*. More sophisticated editors may offer full screen editing facilities, and automatic input and output.

3.5 APPLICATION SOFTWARE

Application programs are written individually, to operate specific tailor made procedures and systems, such as sales ledger system, wares systems, stock inventory systems, library circulation control systems, word processing system etc. Some application programs are available on the commercial market- place as packages. In some applications there are a number of requirements that are common to a number of different users.

Common types of software packages of interest to information managers are:

- Business software
- Database software and database management systems
- Text information management systems
- Library management software
- Communication software
- Expert systems

As we are concerned with the libraries, only the library management software is being dealt within a little detail.

3.6 LIBRARY MANAGEMENT SOFTWARE

Library Management software is specially designed to control the basic activities of a library. Thus, a typical library management software will offer a number of modules:

- **Ordering and acquisitions** – to control the ordering and acquisition of new stock.
- **Cataloguing** – for the maintenance of the catalogue database.
- **Circulation control** – to control the circulation of stock, dealing with issues, returns, borrower records, reservations and fines.
- **Online Public Access Catalogue** – OPAC offers an interface to the catalogue database so that user can search the database.
- **Serial control** – to control all processes associated with serials such as ordering, acquisitions, cataloguing, binding and circulation.
- **Additional modules** – might also support interlibrary loans, management information and community information.

3.7 LIBRARY AUTOMATION

It is the application of computers and utilization of computer based products and services in the performance of different library operations and functions or in the provision of various services and production of output products.

Automation implies a high degree of mechanization where the routines and repetitive jobs or operations are left to be performed by machines with little or no intervention by human beings. Lesser the degree of human intervention, greater the degree of automation. This does not mean that automation does away with human beings. On the contrary human beings are relieved of routine chores giving them more time for tasks which require their intelligence.

In view of the various features of a modern computer system we find that it has been applied in several areas of library work. Book acquisitions, cataloguing, serials control and circulation, information retrieval and dissemination, inter library loan, cooperative acquisition and cataloguing have been automated in libraries.

Efficiency

Librarians are required to answer questions like:

- How many books are checked out by person X?
- Can you compile lists of materials on this or that subject?
- How many books are overdue? Who has them?
- How much time is required for cataloguing, typing and sorting cards?

It is necessary; though time consuming, to count circulation cards to generate such statistics. With automation the librarian can answer all such questions with little effort.

Productivity

Computers are powerful tools for doing repetitive, time consuming and tasks. When coupled with excellent software, they are the perfect tools for making work in the library easier and more productive. Librarians can have additional time to work with library users to help them find new ways the library can help them.

Access

Computers are excellent research assistants. They can help users find materials that would otherwise be undiscovered on the shelves. For years, librarians have laboured to make their materials accessible through subject, title, and author entries via printed catalogues. Analytic entries provided access points above and beyond the title and author. Now, Library Software on your computer can provide you with even greater access by allowing you to search annotation, summary, and note fields as well as tracings and analytic entries. Software makes possible search by any part of the names of authors and illustrators. Wildcard matching of letter patterns provide additional access points impossible via traditional card catalogues.

Features

Library users of all age groups and of varied backgrounds find Computer searching truly amazing and quick. Due to OPAC (online public access catalogues), the holdings of the whole library are available to them. Librarians appreciate the statistical reports that show circulation by day, week, month, or year. The ease of use ensures that librarians don't spend months training their staff on the use of the computer. On-line help is available throughout Library Software. By incorporating the bibliography reports into the OPAC system, the librarian is freed from the tedious compilation.

3.7.1 AREAS OF APPLICATION

The computers are being applied in the following areas:

Acquisition

A computer based acquisition system involves at least two files. The main file contains the names and addresses of booksellers used by the library. The second file serves to specify the full details of the bookseller with each order, so that; a code number can be used on the order record. These are the main files for Acquisition System:

1. **Vendor file**—the vendor file should generally contain the following data elements:
    - Vendor code number
    - Vendor's name
    - Address
    - Telephone numbers
    - Telex number
    - Gram
    - Currency accepted

2. **User file** — it is essential, because the user no. is to be recorded in the order file. Whenever the document is received from the vendor the user should be posted with this information. The user file generally consists of the following data-elements:
   - User number
   - User's name
   - User's address
   - Telephone no.
3. **Order file—creating purchase order** —All libraries send an order form of some kind to the bookseller. The order system has to receive the new orders into the order file and prepare order forms.

Ordering the Items

The first output of an order system is printing of an appropriate "order form" to the supplier. Here the created order file is matched with the vendor file by comparing the vendor code and then finally the orders are printed vendor wise. The order forms are duplicated by the system as to the number of copies required by the institution.

Sending Reminders

After the order is placed; it is expected to be supplied within the stipulated period. If no information regarding the order is received within this period, an appropriate reminder is generated and sent to the vendor. The number of reminders to be sent and the interval between two reminders is also predetermined.

Cancellation and Reordering

If the order is not delivered even after reminders the order has to be cancelled and reordered with another vendor.

Accessioning

When the item is received, the accessioning has to be done. The entry in order file has to be transferred to the "accession list file" and certain other data elements are added to the entry. Items got by exchange, gift etc. are also to be added to the accession file. The accession file is used for generating "list of additions" notification to the user, shelf list and also catalogue record.

Accounts

The system should be able to

- Give a fund account report
- Report the matter to the accounts officer

- Send letters to banks for foreign exchange drafts
- Vendor performance report
- Notification to user

By Products

- List of additions
- Catalogue

Cataloguing

The catalogue of a library is the most important record. A good catalogue enables users and library staff to effectively utilize the library's resources. The cataloguing function requires the professional skills of a cataloguer and clerical skills such as typing of main entry cards, duplication of cards, typing of headings, sorting of cards and alphabetization, filling etc.

The following operations in the cataloguing department can be computerized:

- Preparation of catalogue cards
- Preparation of authority file/subject heading list
- Arrangement of catalogue cards in the required sequence for filing or any other purpose
- Preparation of shelf-list
- List of catalogue items
- Centralized and cooperative cataloguing system, list of holdings or printed catalogues

Periodicals

Serials present several problems in their acquisition such as:

- Frequency of publication may change
- Delays in publishing of issues
- Set of issues may be combined into a single issue
- Supplements to some volumes may be published
- Publication may cease
- Publisher may change

In view of these problems an automated serials control system is expected to have the following capabilities:

- Monitor the expiry of journal subscription and send out renewal order
- Ensure that issues received are properly registered
- Send out reminders for issues not received but are overdue
- Prepare list of serials by vendors and/or publishers
- Prepare list of duplicates and wants for exchange purposes
- Maintain records of payments, expenditures and budgets by fund
- Prepare routing slips for journal issues
- Enables updating of holdings list
- Prepare list of serials ready for binding

Circulation

Major components of circulation system are:

- **Book record**
  In this file the bibliographic records of the books or items of information available in the library are stored.
- **Borrower's record**
  In this file detail of the borrowers such as their names, designations and addresses restored.
- **Daily transactions record**
  This file is expected to answer the following questions.
  - Books issued to a particular reader
  - Books overdue with a particular reader
  - Total number of books overdue and total fine
  - Search of book by a particular author
  - Search of book by a particular title
  - Search of book on a particular subject
  - Number of books issued per day
  - Number of books returned per day
  - Total number of book transactions per day
  - Total number of book transactions cumulated fortnightly, monthly, yearly etc.
  - Total number of transactions in a particular subject field.

3.8 INFORMATION STORAGE AND RETRIEVAL (IRS)

The enormous growths in the volume of published literature and increasingly specialized nature of the literature have resulted in serious problems in accessing information that is retrieving information.

Many secondary services such as abstract journal appears in order to facilitate search-ability and brows-ability of the increasing volume of information were becoming numerous. Further indexes to these journals were not adequate as required by specialist users.

The use of computers to store a large body of bibliographical of other information with the capability to search a DATABASE in a multidimensional manner particularly by subject has become an important application. Systems, which permit such access, are called *INFORMATION.*

The software for IRS enables the definition of a database, search of the database by several parameters and the production of various information products and services. Software for IRS is available for mainframe.

IRS for bibliographical applications is generally characterized by the fact that they permit very large record sizes, search capabilities and flexible output formatting.

Use of computers for IR was first time demonstrated in 1960s. Manual or semi-manual searching of literature in the field of science and technology was becoming impossible for the librarians and the users as it was time consuming but never exhaustive.

It has been seen that in addition to routine house keeping activities, libraries and information centers are now concentrating on IR services in a big way. After quick acquisition and processing of documents through computerized systems the focus is to retrieve and disseminate of transfer the required information instead of documents to the users by repackaging it in a desired and speedy manner, speed and efficiency are the two important criteria of such IRS. It can be achieved by using computers and online information services.

REFERENCES

1. Emery, G – Elements of Computer Science, New Delhi: BPB, 1991.
2. German, G E ed. – Digital Factor in Library and Information Service, London: Facct, 2002.
3. Haung, Samuel, T – Modern Library Technology And Reference Services, New York: Hawerth Press, 1993.
4. IGNOU – BLS Course Reading booklets, New Delhi, 2004.
5. Lasselle and Ramsay – ABC's of IBM PC and Compatibles, New Delhi: BPB,1990.
6. NIIT – Computer Overview and DOS, New Delhi: NIIT, 1997.
7. Pace, Andrew, K – The Ultimate Digital Library, Chicago: American Library Association, 2000.
8. Peterson, Ann and Nancy, A, ed.- Digital Library Use, London: MIT Press, 2003.
9. Rajasekhar, TB – Computer Software for Library and Information Work: Problems and Prospects for Indian, *IN* IASLIC Bulletin, Vol. 32, No. 4, 1986.
10. Tripathi, SM – Documentation and Information Services and Networks, Vol. 2. Information Systems and Networks, Agra: Y.K. Publishers, 1997.
11. Satyanarayan, NR – Manual of Library Automation and Networking, Lucknow: Royal Book Agency, 2004.

12. Srivastava, Rajeeva – Application to Library Software Packages, An Evaluation, Lucknow, 1995.
13. Vashishth, CP ed. – Computerisation and Library Network, New Delhi: ILA, 1991.
14. Verma, R – Guide to Successful Computerization, New Delhi: BPB, 1990.
15. Webb, Terry, D – Professional Issues at Library Automation, London: Hawerth Press, 2000.
16. Websites: infolibrarian.com, informindia.co.in, libraryworld.net, library.geac.com, librarysoftwares.net, web.inflibnet.ac.in, mcitconsortium.nic.in, oclc.com, info.com/ librarysoftware, multiplayergames.in.

CHAPTER 4

LIBRARY MANAGEMENT SOFTWARE PACKAGES

A large number of Library management software packages are available in the software industry. Some of them consist of an integrated set of modules like acquisitions, cataloguing, circulation, serials control, OPAC etc. while others are independent modules meant for automation of single functions.

The Library management software taken in this part is neither definitive nor complete; it is only a representative list of different types of modules available. Special features of some of the software packages is discussed under the following categories.

4.1 Software for specific housekeeping jobs
4.2 Software for information storage and retrieval
4.3 Software for integrated library systems

4.1 SPECIFIC HOUSEKEEPING JOBS

Software packages are versatile in nature. When any package is adopted the whole computer installation costs vary much and it is always tried to automate the whole system by using a single package. But this cost aspect has not hampered the development of software packages especially developed for performing specific task of the library such as acquisition, circulation, serial control, cataloguing, reference etc. Some software packages are included in this chapter under the name of task they are particularly related with. Those software packages are listed below:

4.1.1	Acquisition	:	INNOVACO
4.1.2	Cataloguing	:	LASS (Microcomputer) , ELHILLIII.C The edit software,
4.1.3	Circulation	:	Integrated Library System;
4.1.4	Serial Handling	:	Meta Micro Library System Class Checkmate, PACS,

4.1.5 Data Base Management : CONDOR, TDM SOFTWARE, dBase III, The IV + V System software package.

4.1.1 ACQUISITION

I. INNOVACQ Software

INNOVACQ Software package has been developed by Innovative Interface, the library automation company to integrate the bibliographic networks (OCLC, RLIN, and UTLAS) with circulation system such as CLST LIBS 100 and has been installed as acquisition and serials control system in the libraries across the country. The University of Michigan at Ann Arbour and Michigan State University has installed INNOVACQ.

It is a turnkey acquisition system. The Innovative Interface Inc. provides microcomputer with hard disk. The Software is written in Pascal language.

Features:

1. The system accepts OCLC records and uses them as the basis of order processing
2. It provides automatic detection of duplicate records with an override for Intentional duplicates
3. The "On-order" and 'in process' files can be searched by author, title, series and locally specified identification fields;
4. Automatic claiming and vendor performance report facilities are also available
5. The system has a fund accounting subsystem and has an interface to allow integration with external accounting system.

With the help of this software package any modern library can automate the acquisition section. The most important factor, which can be counted, is that, it is suitable for online function also.

4.1. 2. CATALOGUING

I. Lass Microcomputer Software

LASS software developed by Gory Strewn of North Western University. This new system was an improvement over the older method of individually typing each authority card and cross-reference. University of Arizona Library was one of several libraries selected to perform a final test of the LASS authority software. They're the use of OCLC M 300 and the Lass software to download and print library of Congress Name Authority records has made authority work more efficient and less costly.

LASS software follow OCLC formats authority records into printed cards.

Hardware Requirement

It is a microcomputer-based program that runs on IBM or compatible personal computers. It can be run from two floppy disks or a hard disk. Memory requirements are a minimum of 320 K RAM. Input to the system is from two sources.

System Overview

Authority records are downloaded from OCLC using the save screen function of the M 300. These records can be edited either before they are downloaded or after conversion into LASS records. Locally created records can also be keyed in using a menu driven work form.

Output consists of alphabetized printed authority cards and cross-references for multiple locations. MARC records can also be created for external storage for archival use or can be exported into another database. One important distinction is worth emphasizing. The system is not designed as a local authority file. Once the records are processed they are deleted from the files.

Training can be accomplished easily. It was found that it takes two hours sessions for clerical staff to become independent users.

LASS represent an important step towards more efficient operation of a catalogue department in a card environment. Errors on cards virtually non-existent since keying are minimal.

II. ELHILL III C Software

The National Library of Medicine USA uses this software. The hardware needed for this software package is IBM 2780. Through any Tele type compatible terminals the users can access to BLAISE system database in real times using ELHILL software. The software is well known and well documented. It will enable users to retrieve records very easily from the MARC and MEDLARS files and to have the records output either online through local visual display units or printers or offline for printing and dispatch to users overnight.

System Overview

Certain data elements from the record will be available for searching in the BLAISE system. For the MARC file, data elements will be selected from the fields and put into an index file, which can be searched. This index file will contain control numbers including ISBN, LC Card Number and BNB Number; classification codes, author names; works taken form the title of the item and subject headings.

This inverted file structure of the ELHILL system is visible to the user through use of the 'NEIGHBOR' command. The user of the 'NEIGHBOR' command will be shown a portion of the alphabetical with the retrieval software so that users will be able to move easily from the retrieval sub-system to the edit subsystem and back again.

Features

When the user has found some references in the system that he desires to use for creating his own catalogue or for another local activity, he can have the relevant records transferred to the edit subsystem. The records will be copied onto an on line transient file and will be help in that file for the user to manipulate as he wants. Thus effectively, the records will be the users and his alone.

When he has finished manipulating the data in records, the user will be able to have them output by way of off-line output facilities mentioned above. He will also be able to have displayed or printed using his own terminal in on-line mode.

One of the features to be incorporated in the system is a filter or screening device'; which can be specified by the user. Whereas the records taken from the retrieval sub-system will be full MARC records, records taken into the edit sub-system will be automatically stripped the fields which the user doesn't want, so that he will be able to have transmitted to the edit web-system the exact form of the record to meet index file. For example, If the user puts in the work FRANCE the NEIGHBOR command will show him that the term occurs as a MELARS index term, (MH) 1763 times, as a place of publication (PL), 1222 times and as various authors (AU) once Each. In this way, the user can see precisely how the bibliographic items have been indexed and can select appropriate terms or spellings of terms to use for retrieval. He can also say whether wants to see all term in the index file or just those corresponding to one date-file.

A further feature of ELHILL is the 'SIRING SEARCH' capability, which enables the user to search in a serial fashion for any data elements in the full record. This technique is valuable if a user has already retrieved a set of about one hundred references using the normal index terms, he can refine his search economically through the 'STRING SEARCH' facility to select a subset containing a specific sequence of character such as a phrase or publishers imprint.

Apart from on-line output, there will be a variety of options for off line out put of records. These include the normal off-line print facilities as well as the off-line search capability in ELHILL, so that users can select records and carry out off-line searching overnight when it is cheaper.

III. THE EDIT Software

THE EDIT software is being written specifically for BLAISE and will be integrated his own cataloguing requirements. Users can use this device to create mini-MARC records containing selected fields for output from the system. The user will obtain access to individual records in the sub files either through a system-generated BLAISE number which is unique record identifier within the system or through use of positioning commands; or by working serially through the files to find out the record he wants. When he locates the record, he will be able to amend individual fields in the MARC record, using very simple edit commands. The display will show a field code with a print qualifier. Thus the user can alter the tag number as well as the data. New records can be created in a very similar fashion and a variety of aids, including prompt commands, will be provided. The user in this profile can specify the prompt. There will also be macro commands, which will enable users to store routing editing commands and recall them.

The edit sub-system has a command which will enable users to copy a record from any sub-file onto any other sub-file including within the same sub-file. This will help users willing to exchange records or wanting two copies of records so that they can create two similar records. Users can keep their records in the online transient file for as long as they please but the cost of holding records for more than one month will deter them. This facility will be useful for users wishing to hold a record until it has been checked.

The user can dispatch information from the file by one or more output option, so that he can ask for an off-line print for checking and subsequently have the date output on magnetic tape.

4.1.3 CIRCULATION SYSTEM

I. Integrated Library System (ILS)

ILS is designed by Listed Hill National center for biomedical communications of the NLM. Which is system running on larger microcomputers such as DEC's LSI H/23 using the MIIS (Meditate Interpretive Information System) operating system.

System Overview

The software package includes a master bibliographic file (MARC format), a circulation module, a periodical control module and a search module. The circulation module is table-driven and the system parameters such as loan periods, fine rates etc. may be specified and charged whenever needed. Many terminals can be connected and used, Charging and discharging use light pens for recording bar codes, with manual keying facility for override.

The system has facilities for recall, renewal and reservation according to various operators prescribed parameters. The system provides for automatic renewal of all documents borrowed by a particular user using a single command. Documents returned are stored on a 'Cart'- a particular storage area. When the documents are returned to the shelves the 'cart' is emptied by a single command and the location field is updated to the proper shelf location.

The readers file allows updating and inquiry by name or identification no. of the reader, the usage statistics by readers is also maintained. The transaction file is tied (Linked) to the master bibliographic record and it can be accessed using identification number, author, call number and title. The master bibliographic file can also be accessed by ISSN, ISBN, LC card number and subject.

The system provides outputs such as recall notices, over-dues and fine billing. It can also produce bibliographies and SDI bulletins request. Other reports produced include documents, and reader status reports (such as overdue documents, delinquent borrowers), usage analysis and new acquisition costs. An interface to the online computer library center is provided to allow operators to capture bibliographic information directly from ODLC. The software is available from NTTS.

4.1.4 SERIAL HANDLING

I. META MICRO Library System

This is the periodical control system offered by Meta Micro Library system Inc., is a turnkey system with Hardware and software.

Hardware Requirement

It uses the southwest Technical products 3 = microcomputer having internal memory 128KB to 1 MB using Motorola 6809. The system uses Winchester hard disks 16MB; and 32 MB-1. It also has a tape for backup copy. Terminal (1 to 5) and dot matrix printers (1 to 3) are provided as other peripherals. The system written in Pascal runs on UNI FLEX operating system.

System Overview

The system can handle from 3000 to 8000 titles. The database uses full MARC record. The maximum record length is 9000 characters. The maximum number of fields per record is 115. The database can be searched using up to 12 keys in Boolean combination. At registering, the system recognizes duplicate issues received and provides a list of duplicate issues for exchange purpose Late/missing issues are automatically claimed subject to review by the operator. Routing slips are also printed. Full binding control is provided with binding slips, claiming and payment of bindery invoices etc.

New subscriptions are handled by the ordering module, several other reports are provided by the system including budget, daily activity etc.

II. CLASS CHECKMATE Software

The periodical control system checkmate has been developed by the California Library authority for system and services (CLASS). This software package runs on TRS-80 model II using 8-inch floppies. The system is written in BASIC language.

It can support unto 2000 records, which may be expanded to 6000 record if required. In addition to registering and automatic claiming for late/missed issues, the system can prepare routing slip up to 250 people. The accounting module can calculate and display expenditures for all subscriptions charged and provide totals. The database contains MARC-like or user defined field tags. The user can define which fields are needed. To indelicate temporary constraints on a subscription, notes can be added to records and deleted when not needed. It provides automatic check system for claims.

The database is searchable by Boolean combinations of keywords and defined field. The printed lists of the database can be generated in required formats defined by the operator. It can print the list of periodicals based on title or subject. It keeps details of holding and subject.

Hardware Requirement

The system has been upgraded and can run on any microcomputer with 64k internal memory running under TRS DOS, PC DOS, MS DOS or CP/M operating systems.

III. PACS Software

PACS stands for Periodical Acquisition Control System. PACS is being computerized at the IIM's Computer Center (Indian Institute of Management, Lucknow). It has been developed to run on a mini computer (SN 73). SN 73 system has 2 MB main memory; a 168 MB Winchester disk drive; 1 vacuum column tape drive for maintaining the back; One dot matrix printer and one line printer. Personal computer where PACS can be run has 512-KB main memory; 2 floppy disk drives; a 20 MB Winchester disk drive and a dot matrix printer.

In order to be very familiar with the various inputs and outputs necessarily required for the automated PACS, the system was divided into five subsystems:

(i) **Selection System**

Periodicals recommended by the competent users are selected for ordering/renewal/cancellation subject to the following:

(a) The financial resources of the library;

(b) The scope of the library;

(c) The periodicals already being subscribed by the library; and

(d) The demands of users of the library.

(ii) **Acquisition System**

Periodicals are acquired through any one or more of the following means:

(a) subscription/renewal ordering though publishers/agents;

(b) by becoming embers of various societies/learned association;

(c) by exchange; and/or

(d) by gift or on complimentary basis.

(iii) **Payment System**

This subsystem takes care of checking and passing of bills.

(iv) **Control System**

Some of the different kinds of controls imposed on the periodical acquisition system are:

(a) control at placement of the order;

(b) control at the sending of the reminder to supplier for bills;

(c) control at payment of the bills;

(d) control at the receipt of the initial issues;

(e) control at the receipt of the regular issues;

(f) control at the receipt of the title/contents/index pages;

(g) control at the sending of the reminder to suppliers for issues;

(h) control at the receipt of supply from binders;

(i) control at input of valid date.

(v) **Binding System**

A list of periodicals ready for binding is generated at the desired intervals and the sets are sent to the binders for binding. After the bound periodicals are received; the same are accessioned. This system includes the generation of the lists indicating;

(a) Periodicals ready for binding;

(b) Bound periodicals received in a specific period from the binders.

(vi) **Inputs & Output**

For a computerized PACS some input information is required related to each periodical. The input information required to the processed to generate different output reports/statements.

4.1.5 DATABASE MANAGEMENT SYSTEM

I. CONDOR Software (a specialist language dictionary database)

The CONDOR package, marketed as relation DBMS, consists of around 50 individual programs, (e.g. DEFINE, DBMS, SAVE, SORT and UPDATE). Each customer is given a license number, which has to be typed in every time that the package is used.

Hardware Requirements

To run condor series 20 az-90 micro-computer with at least 48 k RAM or on intel-8086 based microcomputer (16-bit with 128k RAM is needed running either cp./M, 86 or MP/M.

Condor is available in three versions, version I allow single file handling; it has full screen formatting, computation and POST facilities but cannot handle multiple files. Version 2 allows multiple files using the PROJECT and JOIN facilities, versions 3 adds indexing and fuels report writing facilities. Particulars features of version three include a date dictionary system (which provides synonyms for date base names as well as different entry and display formats for the same date set), transaction processing for efficient updating of a master file, sorting of unto 32 date items, selection of records using unto 32 logical conditions (Boolean operation AND, OR and NOT) and JOIN and COMPARE commands for relating two databases on specified matching data items.

It is user friendly as it has English like command language, which is fairly easy to understand. As far as response time is concerned it will take more time when large data will be handled. Despite claiming to be a relational database the records are searched sequentially.

In common with many DBMS, condor is not ideally suited to text handling. Naming a field limit of 127 characters is particularly restrictive for long titles. Condor is suitable for small collection of data.

II. TDM Software (For Library Database and Statistical Analysis)

TDM stands for 'The Data Machine' is a general-purpose database management and reporting system designed for files resident on hard disk system. It requires an Apple ii microcomputer with the Pascal language system an 80-column display and either three floppy disk or a corpus hard disk system TDM has been used to handle catalogue of periodical holdings and of video recording at the central polytechnic library, Lancaster.

TDM allows unto 32 767 records with a maximum 512 characters per record. The maximum no. of fields per record are 40 and the maximum length of a field is 60 characters. The system permits restructuring of the database records to accommodate additional, expanded or deleted fields. Each individual record can be accessed by a primary key. There can be records having the same key. Secondary index dye to leaches records can be all or selected portions of any data fields. Reports can be generated using soured keys of 27 character long. The sort key can be any or combination of selected portion of any fields. The selection and retrieval of records can be effected using Boolean logic statements of unto 480 characters. The search strategies can be saved for future retrieval.

Periodical database contains 3300 records of 425 characters long. The video recordings database contains 2500 records of 498 characters each. The timings for selected operations on the periodical database are as follows:

(1)	Add 10 new records	4 m 22s
(2)	Replace 1 field in 10 records	2 m 12s
(3)	Print full data base 3300 records	2 hrs 24 m
(4)	Sort on 1 field 1000 records	32 m 18s
(5)	Select and print 200 records by matching	43 m18s
(6)	Complete back up of 20 MB disk on	40 m disk

The software has facility to select related records from two or more databases or sequential riles to create a new database or sequential file.

Databases are created and maintained within TDM using the program TDM UPDATE. As this is the program within the TDM package that is used most frequently, TDM UPDATE is set under the constipation software to lead and run automatically for all library applications based on TDM.

The software is relatively robust and extremely flexible. The database structure for updating gives a very simple mechanism for creating and maintaining files on-line, TDM UPDATE would be improved by the inclusion of a facility to design screen formats for the display of records during the updating process. The report with TDM REPORT used in conjunction with free text selection criteria, provides a powerful and flexible approach for processing data, although the maximum sort key length of 25 characters is often rather restricting.

Little previous specialist knowledge or training is required for the use of TDM. The facility to restructure a database at any stage has enabled applications to develop gradually, incorporating new ideas as they arise. As it is simple to produce a text file form a TDM database data currently held within TDM can easily be converted for other software packages as required in the future. TDM is not designed for multiple on line access using a variety of approaches. Secondary indexes have to be built by creating and sorting a tag file as a batch process.

III. THE IV+V System Software

It has been developed by the institute for machine documentation (IMD) GRAZ, Austria and called IV+V System (Information Vermittlung and Vararbeitung information procurement and processing). It is conceived as a generalized database management system intended for bibliographic and factual information management. It is designed as an implementation of the relational database model.

The system has got following capabilities

- Creation, updating, correction and maintenance of local databases
- Data validation on the basis of specified criteria

- Boolean combination search with truncation and adjacency check
- Creation of various outputs-bibliographies, directories etc.
- Connection of host systems through communication channel, and
- Data output on various storage medium.

The system also includes a screen processor which permits user – developed screens and user – controlled screen sequencing for specific a applications and a task schedule, which provides operating system control of tasks, all database management systems and utility software is written in UCSE Pascal, this system functions only in single-use mode and in this context is available for use on IBM PC-AT Wang PC and DEC Rainbow microcomputers as well as the DEC PDPII series using the single user operating system RT-II.

This system is under active consideration of IN-SCO for using portable software package for information handling and they are preparing a demonstration database on its microcomputer using IV+V and implementing and common communication format (CCF). UNESCO is negotiating for making the developed system available to developing countries.

IV. dBase III Plus Software

dBase plus is a data base management system, produced by ASHTON-TATE, USA, it is a revised and an enhanced version of a BASE III software, it is also called relational database management system.

It helps in collecting and managing information of data in the form of database (file). It will help one to design database files as per requirements and according to the specific format. One can edit, view, change data in the database through easy-to use commands. Once the database is ready, one can use it retrieve selected information from it and print reports as per the desired format. The best part is that the data stored in the database is flexible, i.e. one can change/modify the contents as well as the structure of a database any number of items. It is very simple to learn and use. Only a single command can list or print reports, replace contents of a particular field in the entire database. Besides these multiple database files. It can also be used in local area network where several persons work simultaneously on different computers on a single of different applications.

Hardware Requirements

dBase III plus runs today's most popular PC, i.e. IBMMM PC, PC——XT, PC-AT or 100% IBM compatible computers on PC-DOS version 2.0 or MS-DOS version 2d.11 jor higher. .pa

Hardware requires –

1. At least 384 k bytes RAM.
2. Two 360 bytes floppy drives, or one floppy drive and one hard disk.
3. Any printer, at least 90 columns wide.

Technical Specifications

Field sizes:

- Character fields – 1 to 254 bytes;
- Data fields – 8 bytes;
- Numeric fields – 19 n/bytes maximum;
- Memo fields – 5000 bytes maximum

System Overview

File operations:

(a) There can be a maximum of 15 open files of all types.
(b) There can be a maximum of 10 open files termed as database files.
(c) A database file can have up to seven open index files.
(d) Only one format file can be open per active database file.
(e) Each database file can be related to only one database file.

Memory variables

- Types character, Numeric, Logical and date.
- Up to 256 memory variables can be defined, subject to a maximum of 6000 bytes used to store them.
- Character variables can be 1-256 characters longs.
- Nine bytes are used to store a data/numeric type memory variable.
- Logical variables require two bytes of memory.

Database files

- Fields/record-128 maximum
- Records/file-1 billion maximum
- Records/size-4000 bytes maximum
- File size- 2 billion bytes maximum

Miscellaneous

- The command line can be up to a maximum of 254 characters long;
- Any number of spaces can be used between the words of a command (subject to a maximum of 254 characters per command line);

- dBase commands can be abbreviated to the first four characters, e.g. the MODIFY COMMAND can be abbreviated MODI COMM;
- dBase commands, functions, fields names etc. can be typed in upper case, lower case or any mixture of letters;
- The system of the dBase commands can be entered in any sequence.

Features

- dBase 3 plus contains all the dBase 3 commands and functions, plus additional command and features. It is more user friendly;
- It can run on the LAN. Therefore it can now be used for applications such as on-line Reservation system information Retrieval system, Banking etc. Database files can be now protected through PROTECT utility so that only authorized users have access to the database files. These features are available on the Network version of dBase 3plus. Which is called the dBase ADMINISTRATOR;
- Program files can now be created through some sort of command to a form so that others cannot see or modify the program some code listing. This helps prepare marketable application progress in the dbase programming language which run but cannot be modified;
- The data stored in the dBase 3 plus files can be transferred to other software programs/formats e.g. WordStar/Lotus BASIC BASICA or GWBASIC Multiplan, vesicle, SDF, SYMPHONY etc. similarly files from these software/programs/ formats can also be read into dBase 3 plus;
- It does not have any built in command/function for be used to achieve limited graphics capabilities. It can set the user view the database file in a particular way.

4.2 INFORMATION STORAGE & RETRIEVAL

Software packages for information storage and retrieval are meant for developing database of particular type of information exhaustively covering the data on specific fields e.g. Technology, biomedicine, social sc. etc. No matter whether such software are used by national or international databases, they must provide online facilities.

Some of such types of software package included in here are –

4.2.1 ASSASIN
4.2.2 MICRO CAIRS
4.2.3 MORPHS
4.2.4 STAIRS
4.2.5 DIALOG

4.2.6 SCI-MATE
4.2.7 STAR
4.2.8 REFLES

4.2.1 ASSASIN SOFTWARE

ASSASIN stands for Agricultural System for the Storage and Subsequent Selection of Information. This package, although designed and used by ICI's Agricultural Division (Imperial Chemical Industry) is not limited to processing agricultural information but includes facility for batch retrospective searching.

Inputs

The ICI pharmaceuticals division subscribe to form external databases. Records from each database are "sieved" before merging into one file in order to minimize storing multiple copies of the same references. All records are then connected to the format necessary for using ASSASIN. So input to the package can be from a variety of sources such as

- Published serials;
- Patents;
- Internal reports;
- External databases or library accessions.

Each input record is formatted into fields such as

- Bibliographic source;
- Author;
- Title;
- Text or abstract, and
- Added terms used for extra indexing terms

The package matches each word in the record against a stop-list and a thesaurus. Words that do not match are printed out for intellectual consideration. Synonymous words are dealt with as described in the previous section on profile construction forms for information retrieval/output:

Assassin makes the information readily available in a variety of forms. The various outputs from the package include –

- SDI service;
- Know (really KWAC) indexes;
- The ability to perform retrospective searches (currently in bench) abd
- A list of structured thesauri
- Abstract file that can be output as a numerical list of obstructs with full bibliographical details.

The package, which consists of 120 CDBOL programs, can be bought or used at ICIS Computer bureau. Many divisions within ICI use the package and it is also used by external organizations.

The greater London council use ASSASIN to run their information service ACOMPLI (CA computerized London information service). The database used is Urban Abstracts, which is produced by the GLS. The SDI service has over 100 profiles and is run every four weeks. The information system runs at RAPRA, which also uses ASSASIN, and was the only non-IGI user of this package till 1971. Documents to be input to the system are studied and a short indicative abstract of about 10 lines is written. The bibliographic details and the abstract are written on to specially prepared ASSASIN input sheets. The information is punched on to paper tape at RAPRA. As well as being used as input the ASSASIN, the punched paper tape is used in the production of the printed RAPRA abstracts journal. The information on punched paper-tape is sent to ICU's bureau where it is processed on an IBM 360/65 computer.

ASSASIN-PC stems form ASSASIN and is essentially a full text retrieval system, which provides a word processor for the entry of documents up to 5000 characters in length. Words or phrases can be indexed, and these can be selected automatically from the text or specified by the operator during input. Search process is based upon balloon operators, it is a user friendly system-and also can provide on-line service.

4.2.2 MICRO-CAIRS SOFTWARE

Micro CAIRS computer Assisted Information/Library Retrieval System. This is software designed at the Leatherhead Food Research Association, Surrey, England. A number of CAIRS systems can be run simultaneously within one computer each for entry, indexing, storage and retrieval of text or numerical data. The system permits four different methods of data entry direct online entry, batch data entry document data preparation and data prepared using external systems word processors, other computer or key to disk system.

Hardware Requirements

The system can run on ACT SIRIOS, Future Technology systems series 88 IBM PC and any other microcomputer using the Intel 80000088 or running under CP/M-86 or; MP/M-86. The internal memory required is 128 K to any larger capacity; upped 15 terminals, 3 printers and 8 tape drives can be handled by the system. A typical configuration with 128 K internal memory and one 10Mb hard disk can handle upped 10,000 records of 250 characters in length.

System Overview

Each CARIRS system can handle upped 15 different databases each having its own record structure, the sauces, passwords etc. Each database can be divided into 52 files and anyone of these files can be selectively searched. The system uses variable length records. For a record the user can define upped 99 fields each variable in length with a maximum length of 200 characters. The maximum record length is 32000 characters. The following parameters can be defined for a field:

a. name of the field;
b. the length allowed on the screen;
c. the maximum length;
d. mandatory or optional field;
e. Field checks (numeric only or alphabetic only etc.)
f. default data to be inserted in case no data is entered;
g. to be indexed or not, if yes using which technique;
h. to be checked against the saris or not;
i. to be decoded or not (expansion of abbreviations, codes etc; and
j. position of the field on the screen.

Once the parameters are set, prompt on the screen while data entry is automatic.

To create the inverted index file the words in the specified fields are selected automatically using spaces as delimiters and checked against thesaurus, if specified so. The inverted index file may also be checked against a thesaurus if needed. Thesaurus has preferred Terms, BT, NT, QT and Macro-Term (TT) and is entered online using a formatted screen structure. Field Decode file (for expanding abbreviations etc) and stop list file can also be created and used.

Search

All search mechanism such as Boolean combinations, right hand truncation, nesting using parentheses, restriction to the field, validation of search terms against thesaurus, automatic expansion of search profiles using BTs, NTs, automatic expansion of search profiles can be saved on disks for SDI services. Serial searching of the records is also possible which allows for searches to be restricted to certain fields, both right and left truncation, number range searching and Boolean combination of search terms. The system also provides the facility of saving the retrieved records, editing them and printing them according to format specifications. The system also provides security at different levels database level, file level etc. It is also possible to restrict the tasks the user may perform and the denies that output may be sent to.

Info/DDC, Washington DC has been awarded rights to distribute the CAIRS and micro CAIRS. Micro CATRS runs on a variety of operating systems including MS-DOS and CP/M-86.

4.2.3 MORPHS SOFTWARE

MORPHS is an intelligent retrieval system an acronym of minicomputer operated retrieval partially heuristic systems. It was originally developed to be a machinated version of a feature card system. Due to the space limitations of a very small computer, a number of routines were introduced initially to save space such as the automatic elimination of plurals, affix and synonym handling. Subsequently these were found to enhance performance and improved versions of these routines from the foundation, notable a general system of cross referencing and word substitution including and attempt to resolve the problem of homographs. To an extent this is merely the reinvention of the Taurus, but the thesaurus is being used in a far more dynamic capacity at both the input and search stages. It happens that this will enable users to improve their searching performance. Some common misspellings and American variants are incorporated and the user is informed if substitutions have to be made. Although the system is still based upon balloon searching, this has been made as flexible as possible, within its obvious limitations, users are prompted with 'HELP' messages and this should make life simple for the novice every effort has been made to insure that typing is minimized. From the very beginning it has always been intended that MORPHS should be user operated user friendly system. One important feature is that once the system has been loaded, the response time is very fast even for words with thousand of postings.

The program is written in FORTRAN, but does not make some use of features from the PRIMOS operating system. For instance, the time-based help-feature is based on a sub-routine available to prime users. The program is MORPHS is an inverted file, albeit with an unusual structure which has been introduced to provide very rapid loading and retrieval. This file can either provide references to document numbers (in MRPRA implementation to over 50,000 documents stored on microfilm) or to parts of documents (at MRPRA one line of the input string is the minimum display) or to abstracts or whole.

Features

(1) Affix handling-due to limitation of space amount of variety in keywords was reduced by eliminating plurals, suffixes and finally prefixed. So searching is done for root term.

(2) Alternative word forms included morphological variants (such as compounds) abbreviations, synonyms, homographs and exceptions to the affix and plural handling routines. It is possible to disambiguate homographs during automatic indexing though an analysis of collocates their thus-bank (financial) collocates with money, finance, teller, pounds, etc.

(3) MORPHS provide positional soles for handling compounds or phrases. In a phrase the initial letters of the words on either side of the word in question are stored as roles. Most prepositional phrases are automatically translated into their non-prepositional equivalents. An important feature of the positional roles is that they only function during the search for single words the roles are ignored.

(4) In everyday uses data are interposed with 'normal' text. Within computerized systems data tend to be segmented from other types of information. In MORPHS data can be handle concepts such as temperature and handless.

(5) In earlier versions of MORPHS all were subjected to separate routines, but in the new version only personal names are treated separately. Control characters are needed to input material (square brackets are used). Name can be identified and tagged during automatic indexing. On searching names can be expressed as on

loading (that is within square brackets), or in their common ways of expressing personal name with initials:

Smith J.W.
Smith J.W.
Smith, J.W.
J.W. smith,

(6) It provides passwords to its users.

4.2.4 STAIRS SOFTWARE

STAIRS stands for storage and information Retrieval system, which is a program product of the IBM Corporation. Whereas the STAIRS system itself is available through IBM on databases are made available by IBM. Rather the user must purchase or lease the STAIRS programs and apply the system either to commercially available data bases or to private databases. STAIRS runs on the customer's own computer.

System Overview

STAIRS consists of two sets of programs:

(a) Utility programs for data base creation and maintenance;
(b) An on-line retrieval system called AQUARIVS, which stands for a query and retrieval interactive utility system. The retrieval function is a multi-user system which develops an effective dialogue with the user. This dialogue leads to the search and eventual retrieval of stored data. STAIRS implementation includes not only a text processing and document retrieval function but also an associated data base management system. STAIRS uses separate modes of operation to handle text and structured data known as the SEARCH and SELECT modes, respectively.

To use the text retrieval system it is necessary to create an inverted file, a text index, and one or more text files. The text file contains the documents using a special format in which the retrieved documents are presented to the retrieval system users. The text index includes pointer to records in the text file, as well as privacy information and formatted data associated with subsets of records in the text file, these formatted data include attributes for which arrange of values can be specified in advance.

The dictionary contains a record for every unique word included in the database. Associated with this entry is a pointer to a list identifying each occurrence of the particular word in the text. The invented file position for the system may also be used to identify words, which are synonymous with a given term. Access to an individual word in the dictionary is obtained by using letter pairs.

The STAIRS retrieval system uses the free text of the documents or document abstracts for search purpose. Documents are found in STAIRS using the SEARCH command. When this command is specified, the search mode is entered. In this mode the user searches the unformatted portions of the records. Data search statement, normally consisting for a term followed by an operator and another term, is assigned a number of the STAIRS system. The following hierarchy of operations is used to process the STAIRS statements:

ADH

SYN

WITH

AND NOT

OR, XOR

With the ADJ performed first, and OR XOR (excessive OR) operations performed last. The XOR operator indicates that a document is selected whenever it contains either is specified terms or both. Parentheses are allowed in order to alter the order in which the operations are performed.

Select Mode

To manipulate structured data, the STAIRS system uses the completely separate SELECT MODE OF OPERATION. In the formatted fields of data normally containing the values of record command is used to operate in a special ranking mode. In the RANK mode the mode the initial search is carryout using the SEARCH mode of operations. Once a document set has been chosen for retrieval using the search mode operations, a ranking of the documents attributes are searchable. The SELECT mode provides new search operate of the documents different from those specified earlier from SEARCH mode AND OR.

Although the search operators may not be mixed between the SELECT and the SEARCH modes, one can use a query number from the SELECT mode as a part of a query statement in the SEARCH mode.

The processing of information in the SELECT mode differs from the typical information retrieval processing. Rather it fits into a framework explicitly used to handle structured information.

Another fracture to STAIRS is its ability to rank the retrieved document according to one of several pre-specified algorithms. The Rank command is used to operate in a special ranking mode. In the RANK mode the initial search is carried out using is SEARCH mode of operations. Once a document set has been chosen for retrieval using the search mode operations, a ranking of the documents can be optioned by assigning values or weights to the individual terms associated with a document.

STAIRS is a uniquely powerful system. It is designed to offer a great deal of flexibility in the sense that it offers all the power of a free text search system in addition to the formatted retrieval capability based on the values of specific attribute fields. However, the STAIRS system may be expensive to use in that it requires a database management's system in addition to the retrieval system. As well as a large storage capability for the term location, frequency, synonym and associated information. Furthermore, the user must have a large IBM computer system available for use.

4.2.5 DIALOG SOFTWARE

DIALOG is the name given to interactive, computer based information retrieval language developed at the Lockheed pale Alto Research Laboratory. The DIALOG system consists of assures of computer programmers which have been designed to make full use of direct access memory devices and VDU's to provide the user a rapid and powerful means of identifying records within a file which satisfy particular information need. The system has been used successfully by Librarians also.

DIALOG provides maximum interaction between the user and the file. The system is based the inverted file system. From the user's point of view DIALOG consists of several plain ENGLISH commands, such as DISPLAY, PRINT and SELECT, which allow him to perform information retrieval functions. The command are so designed that no pre-specified sequence must be followed i.e., the use is free to select any command he considers appropriate for the next step of the records. The command key orientation results in a very simple clerical procedure: depress command key, key in operand date, press TRANS key to transfer the entire message to the computer corrections are made by back spacing and typing over incorrect characters. Following entry of each command, the system responds with information that exits the user in deciding the next steps to take.

There are six fundamental steps, which are more or less followed in any retrieval process by DIALOG.

---

1. Identify and select index term, which characterize the search interest.
2. Coordinate individual terms into concept group.
3. Sample and evaluate intermediate search results.
4. Modify and/or and reds.
5. Output results.
6. Review actual documents.

In DIALOG two commands, EXPAND and SELECT are provided to assist the user in identifying and selecting desired index terms. On form of EXPAND provides a display of the alphabetically near index terms to the term entered together with an indication of the number of citations index by displayed terms are also the number of cross references or related terms associated with each displayed terms. Another form of the EXPAND command allows the user to display the related terms in the same format.

The SELECT command enables the user to contract a list of desired index terms for future reference SELECT entries result in the definition of file subsets which are tagged with set number and are printed out on the terminal hard copy device.

In designing DIALOG, it was desired not only to provide the user amines of reviewing citations within a particular category, but also to allow him to define dynamically his own categories by logically combining the results of several individual categories. This function was provided in the COMBINE command and the searcher can combine any number of citation sets in any logical manner.

The DISPLAY command in DIALOG was designed to allow the user to review the intermediate results. Of several formats available, that most frequency used provides display of the entire citation including all assigned descriptors and descriptive abstract if available. Supplying the full citation not only enables the user to evaluate the relevancy of his search to that point but it also shows him alternative descriptors he can explore or can include fusing the COMBINE command with other previously developed categories.

Two output commands are; PRINT putouts indicated sets of citations to the high speed printer are the computer; TYPE similarly output to the low speed terminal printer.

Provisions have been made in DIALOG for each citation to be associated with a second record; can be abstract or the entire text of a document.

Of more practical interest at the present in interface to automatic equipment. DIALOG has been used with several of the devices, any of which can contain full document text.

In practice, DIALOG provides the user an easy-to-use command language that extends this concept by providing a means of combining subject/categories and by providing the clerical facility for storing. Cumulating, and printing desired citations variety of formats.

In the 1967, in NASA Ames Research Center, California and was used to conduct online searches of the NASA document. Citation collection which at that time numbered some 300,000 records.

This service is operated on an IBM 360/50 at Lockheed Information Services in California. The service is available via TYMENT and TELENT networks.

4.2.6 SCI-MATE SOFTWARE

Sci-Mate software is developed by the Institute for Scientific Information; Philadelphia is software for micro computers. It previews menu-driven searching of awed variety of online databases and the management to textual information.

System Overview

SCI-MATE is a menu-driven command system guides the user through searches on DIALOG ISI, BRS, SOC and MEDLINE databases, making the search capabilities of the host system. With permission form the database producer or vendor bibliography information retrieval with the universal online searcher can be captured in the user's SCI-MATE personal Data Manager.

Personal data manager is a component of SCI-MATE and with the help of this software feature the user can create his or her own databases. The databases can contain any kind of textual information entered from the keyboard or through universal online searcher and transferred automatically to their personal data manager.

For in house database creation data can be entered as free-text or according to one of the 50 templates defined by the users. Each template has up to 20 fields and the maximum length of a record of 1900 characters. Any characters, word of phrase in record can be used for search. Transaction symbol can be used in any position of a search work. Boolean combination search is also allowed. The retrieved records can be stored on specific fields and printed. All the operations are menu-driven.

The microcomputer needed is IBM PC, the vector 3 or 4, the APPLE TRS 80 model or any CP/M 80 or CP/M 86 based system with 64k RAM, using z.80 or Intel 8006 microprocessors with 8 inch floppies.

4.2.7 STAR SOFTWARE

STAR stands for System to Automate Records developed by Chandra Associate Inc. This software package runs on apple micro systems AM/100/T. This is designed for large files and provides up to 2.4 billion bytes of hard disk as storage. The internal memory size required is from 128k to 1024k. An 8.5 inch Mb disk unit and up to 12 disk units of 60 MB each can be attached. The system allows you up to 24 terminals to be connected for online access and communication. The system supports variable length records of up to 500 records.

The software has the following features:

---

1. It allows locally defined record format and input screen format;
2. Has editing capability for adding; deleting or modifying records;
3. Support controlling vocabulary and allows for global changes when vocabulary is revised;
4. Allows for automatic expansion of abbreviations;
5. Allows Boolean combinations search formulation with vested parentless and truncation;
6. Has the facility to store searches for SDI;
7. Allows for searching more than one database;
8. Permits the output format to be tailored for online display of print out;
9. Allows for specified sorts; and
10. Allows for backup copies on videocassettes that can be automated with clock sittings at specified times.

4.2.8 REFLES SOFTWARE

REFLES stands for REFerence Librarian Enhancement System. This is a microcomputer system developed by Bivins and Palmer for providing reference services in the libraries.

System Overview

The system overview as a group of scratch pad allowing users easy storage of new records, alteration of existing records addition of new descriptors and creation of additional pointers to new and existing records.

The system presents the following functions:

---

1. Display thesaurus;
2. Edit thesaurus;
3. Enter new term and text;

4. Delete term and all text;
5. Edit text;
6. Search and display;
7. User change/Log off;
8. Terminal program;
9. Change disk;

The maximum length of a logical record is 2400 character and a descriptor in thesaurus in 35 characters long. The retrieval is through that thesaurus term displayed by keying in their number.

Hardware

The system runs on a TRS-80 using a 2-80 processor with 16k RAM with an additional 32k RAM with two floppy drives.

The same concept has been expanded in REFLINK software package developed by Linkoping University, Sweden. This system uses an ABC-80 microcomputer with 48k RAM, 16k ROM, two floppy drives and a terminal. The programming language used is ABC-80 Basic. The system is menu-driven and is suitable for small databases like ongoing research projects in an institution and the various activities taking places within them, personal files.

4.3 INTEGRATED LIBRARY SYSTEMS

In this part the following software packages are included:

4.3.1 CDS/ ISIS
4.3.2 DELMARC
4.3.3 DELPLUS
4.3.4 GRANTHALYA
4.3.5 LIBSYS
4.3.6 LS/2000
4.3.7 MECSYS
4.3.8 SLIM
4.3.9 WILISYS
4.3.10 SOUL

4.3.1 CDS / ISIS SOFTWARE

CDS/ISIS software stands for Computerised Documentation Service/Integrated Sets of Information System is developed by UNESCO and distributed by NISSAT in India in free of cost with nominal registration fee.

The history of CDS/ISIS goes back to 1971 when UNESCO began to be involved in the development of the information processing software needed for its own newly created computerized documentation service (CDS). Already in 1960s the ILO had developed software known as the ISIS. UNESCO adopted the ISIS of ILO and began to develop the same force use on its IBM mainframe computer. The first version came out in 1975 and the fully developed version 4 of the CDS/ISIS came out in 1983.

A subsequent development in this line accomplished by UNESCO has been the mini/micro computer version can run on relatively inexpensive equipment and was developed with a view to help smaller libraries and documentation centers, specially in developing countries, in having access to the computerized information processing technology. The mini/micro version can work on IBM compatible microcomputers running under MSDOS operating system. The latest version of this software known as CDS/ISIS mini/micro version 2.3 was released in March 1989.

Hardware Requirement

The Mini/Micro version of CDS/ISIS needs a minimum Microcomputer configuration as listed below-

- IBM PC/XT or AT or other compatible equipment with 512 RAM Memory.
- Floppy Disk Unit,
- Hard Disk
- Mono chrome or colour monitor, and
- Printer

Database

The package has integrated a number of different programs into a single program. All these programs are accessible from a main menu. The package allows a database to contain over 16 million records. Each record can consist of desecrate data elements that are stored in fields. Each field is assigned a numeric tag. The unique characteristic of CDS/ISIS is that it is specifically designed to handle fields of varying length.

System Function/Services

The CDS/ISIS is a versatile package, which performs the following functions:

(1) Defining the date bases containing necessary data elements;
(2) Entering new records into a new database;
(3) Modification, correction or deletion of existing records;
(4) Automatic creation maintenance of fast access files for each database in order to maximise retrieval speed;
(5) Retrieval of records by their contents from a given data base through a sophisticated search language;
(6) Displaying the records according user defined formats;
(7) Sorting of records in any desired sequence;

(8) Printing partial or full catalogues using CDS/ISIS integrated programme facility. The above functions, are performed through a set of a major services, classified into two categories; User services and system services, as follows:

User Services given in Main Menu

Micro CDS/ISIS - Ver. 3.07 (c) UNESCO 1993
Micro CDS/ISIS
Change data base
Change dialogue language

- *ISISENT - Data entry services*
- *ISISRET – Information retrieval services*
- *ISISPRT - Sorting and printing services*
- *ISISINV - Inverted file services*
- *ISISDEF - Data base definition services*
- *ISISXCH - Master file services*
- *ISISUTL - System utility services*
- *ISISPAS – Advanced programming services*

*ISISENT	Data entry and Record Editing
*ISISRET	Information Retrieval
*ISIPRT	Production of printed Out-puts
*ISISNV	Inverted Files Maintenance and Utility functions system services-
*ISIS DEP	Definition of new data bases and/or modification of existing database definition
*ISIS UTL	Miscellaneous system utility functions
*ISIS XCH	Facilities for interchanging data with other systems and master file utility functions
*ISIS PAS	advanced programming facility for developing own application programmes and integrating them with CDS/ISIS.

Database Creation

The following four steps are involved in the creation of database according to CDS/ISIS-

1. Definitions of fields in the records of the master file using the field definition table (FDT).
2. Definition of data entry work sheet using the work sheet editor.
3. Definition of the parameters for the generating of printed outputs such as catalogue indexes by using the formatting language.
4. Definition of the fields of the data base to be made searchable through the inverted file by using the field select table.

Advantage

1. The software is available to Libraries free of cost from UNESCO.
2. This is a proven package, which is very versatile for our type of work.
3. The updating and maintenance of the software is sully guaranteed, as UNESCO is its parent body and support.
4. Software is easy to learn.

Micro CDS/ISIS is an advanced non-numerical information storage and retrieval software developed by UNESCO since 1985 to satisfy the need expressed by many institutions, especially in developing countries, to be able to streamline their information processing activities by using modern (and relatively inexpensive) technologies.

The software was originally based on the Mainframe version of CDS/ISIS, started in the late '60s, thus taking advantage of several years of experience acquired in database management software development. Several partners contributed to its development through the years.

The development of the Windows version was the result of strategic development policy decision aiming at maintaining the leading role CDS/ISIS has played and is still playing on the international scene.

Latest official versions

- CDS/ISIS Dos Ver. 3.07
- Winisis 1.5 build 3 (Standard)
- Winisis 1.5 build 7 (Arabic enabled)

The major features of the CDS/ISIS software are:

- The handling of variable length records, fields and sub fields, thus saving disk space and making it possible to store greater amounts of information;
- The handling of repeatable fields;
- A data base definition component allowing the user to define the data to be processed for a particular application;
- A data entry component for entering and modifying data through user-created data base specific worksheets;
- An information retrieval component using a powerful search language providing for field-level and proximity search operators, in addition to the traditional and/or/not operators, as well as free-text searching;
- A powerful sort and report generation facility allowing the user to easily create any desired printed products, such as catalogues, indexes, directories, etc.;

- A data interchange function based on the ISO 2709 international standard used by leading data base producers;
- An integrated application programming language (CDS/ISIS Pascal and the ISIS_DLL), allowing the user to tailor the software to specific needs;
- Functions allowing the user to build relational data bases, though CDS/ISIS is not based over a relational model;
- Powerful hypertext functions allow designing complex user interfaces.

A Windows interface between CDS/ISIS and IDAMS, the UNESCO software for statistical analysis, has also been developed. From the outset, CDS/ISIS was created as multi-lingual software, providing integrated facilities for the development of local linguistic versions. Thus, although UNESCO distributes only the English, French and Spanish versions of the package, user-developed versions exist in virtually all languages, including special versions which UNESCO helped in developing, for Arabic, Chinese and Korean.

Compatibility between the DOS and Windows Versions

No conversion is needed when moving from CDS/ISIS DOS to CDS/ISIS for Windows. However, formatting language functions are just 95% compatible. In some cases you may find some syntax errors appearing: you may have to adapt your display format to the new one. In terms of search engine, the two versions are totally compatible: both can use the same I/F (inverted file). The data entry worksheets are also compatible but the screens will appear different.

Arabic Version

UNESCO and the League of the Arab States (Department of Information and library) developed an Arabic enabled version of CDS/ISIS for Windows.

The latest version 1.5 runs on Win95, Win98, WinMe, 2000 and XP operating systems.

The software comes in three languages: English, Arabic (Egypt) and French. It contains as well an example database in Arabic and English.

The whole user interface is reversed Right to Left when the software starts in Arabic language. A special feature allows the switch from RTL to LTR.

WEBLIS, AN INTEGRATED LIBRARY SYSTEM BASED ON CDS/ISIS

WEBLIS is a Web based Library Integrated System based on CDS/ISIS. The system has been developed by the Institute for Computer and Information Engineering (ICIE), Poland, based on their experience in building library systems for international organizations such as FAO, IFAD and GTZ. WEBLIS runs through the WWW-ISIS engine, also developed by ICIE.

This achievement is also part of the efforts of UNESCO's communication and information sector to encourage FOSS (Free and Open Source Software).

These tools are now distributed by UNESCO free of charge. Soon, the free ware WWW-ISIS engine will be distributed as Open Source software.

UNESCO's CDS/ISIS is one of the most widely used information retrieval software. Beside the main software, CDS/ISIS for Windows, a number of tools are available from UNESCO or other parties in many different languages. In 2004, UNESCO's Secretariat in Paris has satisfied more than 3,000 requests.

The current version of WEBLIS, available in English, consists of the following modules:

- Cataloguing system
  (Books, papers from book, papers from journals, journals, miscellaneous -slides, photos, audio, video, etc.)
- OPAC
  On-line public access catalogue- (basic and advanced search, history, saving queries function, and ISIS Query language facilities, thesaurus based search)
- LOAN module
  (Hold/reserve, loan/ renew, automatic claiming by e-mail or a traditional mail in word form, urgent task lists)
- Statistical module
  (The main goal of the program is to generate statistical data aggregated from the CDS/ISIS databases).

WEBLIS is a freeware, implemented on WWW-ISIS as a platform. Its functionality and user interface is just "coded" by HTML, print formatting language, definition files and HTP files. If you upgrade the system by changing any of those files and would like to include your contribution to the system, please contact UNESCO.

4.3.2 DELMARC SOFTWARE

This software has been developed bearing in mind the size and operations of the libraries. It is designed for bigger libraries that have collections of more than one lakh.

In order to modernize and networked major libraries in India, DELNET presents DELMARC- the Library Management Software that conforms to international standards. The software is ideal for University libraries, Public Libraries and Research Libraries with more collections. It is offered to Member- Libraries of DELNET at a subsidized price.

Special Features

1. Software is Barcode enabled.
2. It is designed and developed exclusively to work in all kinds of libraries including public libraries, academic libraries and special libraries.
3. Multi-user facility allows different branch Libraries/ sections/ nodes of a library to function together.

4. Free upgradation available.
5. Follows internationally recommended standards and formats such as US-MARC, MARC 21, UNIMARC, and UK-MARC.
6. Provision for Backlog Entry.
7. Backup and Restore facility.
8. Provides Lists of Country Codes, Language Codes,
9. Online Help Available.
10. Bar-coded Stock Verification Facility.

DELMARC manages libraries with extensive collections, complex operations and serves a large clientele. This software has been designed after a comprehensive study of different library-related functions performed in different kinds of libraries. This software is easy to work with and offers the following modules at this stage:

- Acquisition
- Cataloguing
- Circulation
- OPAC
- Administration
- Export/Import
- Authority Control
- Article Indexing
- Report Generation

Acquisition

The acquisition module enables library staff to handle the following major functions related to acquisition of library material:

1. Suggestions management
2. Approvals
3. Ordering, Cancellation and Reminders
4. Receiving of Documents
5. Accessioning
6. Management of Vendors, Publishers and Currency Tables

Cataloguing

1. Cataloguing of any type of material in any MARC format using AACR II rules.
2. Category of material like reference special etc. can be defined.

3. The Shelf No. can also be given to the item that will be useful in stocktaking.
4. Cataloguing of Multiple Copies.
5. Copy of record.
6. Backlog Entry facility.

Circulation

1. Takes care of all possible functions such as issue, return, reissue, reservation, etc.
2. Member enquiries and maintenance of the status of material can be handled.
3. Complex functions like fine management for each category of uses and material can also be effectively carried out.
4. Issue, return or reserve item by Accession No. as well as by Title, author, etc.
5. Overdue charges.

OPAC

1. Individual search (by Author, Title, ISBN, ACC no. , Subject, Class no. etc.).
2. Boolean search (Search by Author, Title, ISBN, ACC. NO. Subject, Class No. Etc. in combination with Boolean operators).
3. Special search (for cataloguing purposes).
4. Provides the New Arrivals' list.
5. Online Reservation of new arrivals or other titles.
6. Results can be seen/printed in AACR-II format or any MARC format described above.

Administration

1. Can define the Member Categories, Member Groups, Currencies and their exchange rates, Acquisition Modes, Payment Modes, Material Categories, Miscellaneous Services, Select/ Unselect MARC tags, holidays, user passwords, etc. that will be used throughout the functioning of the software.
2. Administrator can delete data or restore the deleted data like Members' records, Vendors' Records, Catalogue Records, etc.
3. Generation of Report.
4. Allotment of privileges to members.
5. SDI facility.
6. Other operations like Receipt Block Generation, setting the members' Photo File Format.

Export/Import

Export/Import of data into/from any standard MARC format.

Authority Control

Enable to maintain Author, Title, Series and Subject Authorities and links with the records.

Article Indexing

Maintains a database of various articles indexed in the library or collected; from outside sources.

Report Generation

A wide range of reports are generated including Vendors' list Ordered Material, Received Material, Overdue Orders, Missing Items, Written-Off Items, Reserved Items, Issued Items, Members' List (Brief/Detailed), Stock Verification, Reminders, and Intimations, etc. Reports can be generated by Date as well.

Members' /Vendors' Maintenance

1. Can add, edit or delete the Member's/Vendor's data.
2. Member's photo is automatically picked up from the directory once scanned.

4.3.3 DELPLUS SOFTWARE

This software has been developed bearing in mind the size and operations of the libraries. It is designed for all types of small libraries with a collection upto one lakh.

In order to modernize and network the Libraries in India, DELNET presents DELPLUS the Library Management Software conforms to international standards and presents its applications in a user friendly manner.

Special Features

(i) Software is designed and developed exclusively to work in all types of libraries.

(ii) DelPlus is menu driven with Graphical User Interface (GUI). It is a user-friendly tool for the management of libraries.

(iii) It has an effective administration and security system and provides for password both for system Administrator as well as the User.

(iv) Follows internationally recommended formats such as MARC-21, US MARC.

(v) Best for smaller libraries which have collections upto one lakh holding.

(vi) Barcode enabled.

(vii) Reservation facility for materials.

(viii) Online monitoring of the status of material.

(ix) Interactive facility for maintaining Library Inventory/Database.
(x) Generation of reminders and intimation to the Members.
(xi) Generation of reminders to Vender/ Supplier/ Binder, etc.
(xii) Advanced Backup and Recovery system.
(xiii) Online listing of country and language information with related codes.
(xiv) Online Help System for all Modules.
(xv) A wide variety of Search options.

This software is easy to work with and comprises the following modules:

- Acquisition
- Cataloguing
- Circulation
- OPAC
- Article Indexing
- Authority Control
- System Administration

Acquisition

Acquisition module enables library staff to handle the following major functions:

1. Approvals
2. Request/Recommendation/Suggestions
3. Ordering, Cancellation and Reminders
4. Receiving of Materials
5. Accession Register, and
6. Vendor/Publisher/Binder Management facility.

Cataloguing

Cataloguing of books is undertaken in two ways. Either enters directly or after following various steps such as Approval, Ordering, Accessions, etc.

Main points are as follows:

- New Entry.
- Modification of Previous Catalogue Entry.
- Deletion of Catalogue Entries.
- Entry of Multiple Copies.
- View/Search of Catalogue Entries.

- Online Help System
- Online Country Code and Language Code listing for MARC Entry.

The module enable you to catalogue any type of material in MARC 21, US MARC and CCF with AACR II rules.

Circulation

This module takes care of all possible functions such as Issue, Return Reservation, Renewal, etc. Members' inquiries and Maintenance of the Status of Material can be handled. Complex functions like fine management for each category of membership and materials can also be effectively carried out.

The facilities include:

- Online Inquiry System
- Effective Reservation System
- Option for Issue/Return/Renewal/Reservation/Cancellation
- Reminder/Intimation.

OPAC

The OPAC search facility has been provided with seventeen types of search options. There are also three sub options: Exact Match, Partial Match, and Match by first word/character, under the main option.

The search options are as follows:

Authors, Title, ACC no., ISBN, Subject, Call no., Publisher, Language, Country, Publication Year, Duplicate Copies Search, Conference, Series, Keyword, Subject, Location Code, and Boolean Search.

Article Indexing

This module is developed to maintain database of articles. We have given the following two options:

a. Article Entry.
b. Article Search.

Search can be made by Author, Title, Publisher, Subject Headings, Date, Periodical Title, and Translator.

Authority Control

This module enables the user to maintain Author Title, Series and Subject Authorities. There are two options for Authority:

a. Authority Creation – User can Create Authority Records by Author, Title, Series and Subject.
b. Authority Search – User can Search Authority by Author, Title, Series, Subject.

System Administration

Maintaining a complete and full secure administration system in two parts.

System Administration (part –I)

(a) Data Export/ Import from any standard MARC format
(b) Stock Verification – Number of catalogued books and status, Number of lost/ missing, books, Number of damaged books, Number of written off books, Number of existing books. Status of each record is available.
(c) Report Generation – A complex Report Generation Module, every day available for

Acquisition Reports: Approval Report, Request/Recommended Report, Books Ordered, Books Received, Accession Register, Books Rejected.

Circulation Reports: Member Report, Books Issued, Reserved Books, Over Dues, Membership Renewal Notices Report.

Miscellaneous Reports: Books Catalogued, Vendor/Publisher/Binders, Authority Report, New Arrivals, Article Indexing.

(d) Advanced Backup and Recovery System.

System Administration (part –II)

(a) System Administrators Maintenance (with password setting)
(b) User Maintenance Listing (with password setting)
(c) Master Database Entry – For Language Code, Country code, Member Type and Material, Library Information.
(d) Library Resources – Delplus Calculator, Delplus Word Pad, International Information, like – Country Code, Currency, Currency Rate, ISD-Code, Religion, Language, Capitals, etc.
(e) Grant and Revoke Permission – Here Administrator can grant permission to the Operator/User for a particular module.

4.3.4 e-GRANTHALAYA...LIBRARY AUTOMATION PACKAGE

e-Granthalaya the library automation package developed by National Informatics Centre, Bangalore is aimed to suit the requirements of different classes of libraries.

Highlights

- Maintenance of members, groups, roles, basic information & receipts monitoring.
- Periodical subscription, receipt, billing, payment & daily newspaper monitoring.
- Accessioning the books, maintenance of selection committee list, picking the books required by the library from the list, billing & payments for books, stock verification. Issue, return & renewal of books along with tracing of lost books.
- Searching books / periodicals on title, author, publisher or subject heading. Boolean search for books on title, author or publisher.
- Customized help on the package.

Security

- Access controlled through Login and password.
- Built-in privilege groups of users / operating staff.
- Access may be denied through membership module.

Bilingual Capabilities

Works with NUDI 3.0 developed by Ganaka Parishat, Department of IT, Government of Karnataka and ISM 2000/ Leap office developed by CDAC. It can be customized to suit all Indian languages supported by ISM.

Multilingual Capabilities

Works with ISM office 2000 developed by CDAC. Can be customized to suite all Indian languages supported by ISM.

Other Features

Web enabled query system supports search for books and other materials, request for new books, reader view about a book, List of books borrowed, readers' statistics.

Technology

Platform supported

- Works with Windows 98 / Windows XP / Windows 2000 Professional / Windows NT 4.0 / Windows 2000 Server.
- Back end Database : MS ACCESS / SQL Server.
- Bilingual Tool : NUDI 3.0/ISM 2000/ Leap Office 2000
- Multilingual Tool : ISM office 2000.

Features of e-Granthalaya

- User friendly package which needs minimum training.
- Multi user package with database loaded on the server.

- The individual nodes across different departments can share the data from the server.
- Administrators can create/modify/delete users (password protected) with restrictions to handle different modules.
- Using this package, it is possible to store and retrieve data in languages like Assamese, Bengali, Gujarati, Hindi, Kannada, Malayalam, Marathi, Oriya, Punjabi, Tamil and Telugu.
- Circulation is integrated with barcode interface; hence it requires few interactions with the system.
- Search facilities locate books, journals and serials and other materials quickly.
- Guest account allows non-members of the library to have a look into the holdings of the library.
- Contains extensive help facility to guide the users.

Training

NIC regularly organizes "D7- Library Management System" training program to create awareness about "e-Granthalaya" package for Librarians.

Modules of e-Granthalaya

Administration

Maintenance of members records, with password and access to selected modules. Stock verification and budget control etc.

Serials Control

Periodical subscriptions, receipt, billing, payment & daily newspapers monitoring.

Acquisition

Books indenting, picking the books required by the library from the list, placing purchase orders, supply of books, billing & payments for books, accessioning of books.

Circulation

Barcode enabled issue, return & renewal of books along with keeping track of books lost.

OPAC

Searching books/periodicals through title, author, publisher, subject heading, call no, year of publication, series & keywords. Boolean search facilities also are available.

Reports

Commonly used reports like accession register, member registers, and statistical reports are available in this module. These reports can be customised according to the requirements of Libraries.

Web Utilities

These utilities help in browsing the OPAC over internet/intranet. Also few utilities like readers view, books borrowed, readers statistics, request for a book etc. is incorporated.

HELP

Online help for "e-granthalaya" operating procedure. Help window for each operation by pressing F1 key.

Hardware Configuration

System requirements	*Minimum*	*Recommended*
Processor	Pentium	Pentium III
RAM (Primary Memory)	64 MB RAM	128 MB RAM
Hard Disk Capacity	2.1 GB	4.3 GB
Monitor	Colour SVGA(800X600)	Colour SVGA(800X600)
Operating System	Windows 98 & above	Windows 98 & above
Printers	Dot Matrix	HP Laser jet
Barcode reader	None	Should be interfaced with keyboard
Telephone/e-mail	None	Required for web enabled searching.
CD ROM/DVD Drive	CD ROM/DVD drive for installation	CD ROM/DVD drive for installation

4.3.5 LIBSYS SOFTWARE

"LibSys" for library automation is a product of Info-Tek Consultants Pvt. Ltd., New Delhi engaged in providing software solutions for General Insurance and ERP/CRM. Info-Tek has made LibSys a defacto standard for libraries in India. Its acceptance in global market further strengthens its popularity across the country as the most field proven library system in a wide spectrum of libraries with unmatchable depth in functionality and features.

With open system architecture (3-tier) since its inception and its continuous transition from a host multi-user system to Client-Server implementation and finally a total web-based solution, makes LibSys an advanced multidimensional library system. A powerful and user friendly Web-OPAC along with Windows based OPAC, makes it an outstanding choice for a Library system.

LibSys handles Indian languages/scripts using ISM Publisher and GIST of C-DAC. There is an additional 'Unicode' support in LibSys that facilitates handling of both International and Indian languages/scripts.

When it comes to choosing a suitable platform for LibSys implementation - there are many possibilities such as WINDOWS (NT/2000/XP), UNIX (various flavours) and LINUX, giving a feel of open system for expendability and cross migration in future. Besides its own proprietary database handling capabilities, any preferred industry standard RDBMS such as SQL Server, ORACLE, MySQL etc. can be used as a back-end.

For a modern library having Electronic Surveillance Gate based security system installed, the LSmart interface in LibSys supports various self check-out counters; Book drops stations, etc. based on RFID or any other advance technology.

Adherence of LibSys to standards such as MARC and Z39.50 makes it suitable for cooperative networking and resource sharing. As LibSys can handle digital contents along with various multimedia files and electronic resources, implementation of a virtual library is a distinct possibility.

LibSys has an installation base of more than 800 users making it the most field proven software in the country including Universities, Academic Institutions, National Laboratories/R&D Institutes, Corporate, Government, Public Libraries, Colleges, Schools.

LibSys is an Integrated Library Management Software covering almost all the functions of a library in the following areas:

- Acquisition/Ordering
- Cataloguing
- Circulation Serials Control
- Article Indexing System
- OPAC (Online Searching of Bibliographic Information)
- Web OPAC

- Built around its own centralised bibliographic database based on MARC standards, LibSys supports both print and non print materials. LibSys has various formats to describe each material type, using different fields with variable field lengths. It facilitates import/export of data in standard exchange format such as MARC as well as other formats.
- LibSys provides on-line validation of input data prior to updating the database. Prompts and suitable messages are flashed when the data does not match and 'look-up tables' provides help as and when required.
- LibSys supports word based free text searching using Boolean operators. An efficient proprietary indexing feature substantially improves response time while searching for bibliographic information in large databases. The bibliographic database searching is integrated with the Circulation and Acquisition operations.
- In circulation operations, either bar-code or RFID technology may be employed for identification of both borrowers and materials. LibSys permits self check-out, book drop etc. using LSmart interface.
- LibSys implements security by allowing access through passwords. Security is provided for the user as well as for the library staff. For the staff, access can be controlled even at the function level.
- The Java/'perl' based interface in LibSys Web OPAC provides an effective gateway to Internet and Intranet. The Z39.50 compliance in LibSys ensures keeping pace with the developments in international market place.
- LibSys is a powerful software written in 'C / C++' and 'Java' providing extremely user friendly interface during operations. Although LibSys is based on its own Bibliographic database, it is also available for environment using ORACLE (or SQL Server or MySQL) as back-end RDBMS. Full Graphical User Interface (GUI) front-end is provided for the windows client.

- LibSys supports various electronic resources thus making it a modern system with virtual library implementation. Image and multimedia files can be integrated with LibSys search engine. They may be browsed in multi-windows interface with standard window features. Various formats handled by LibSys include Bitmap (.BMP), TIFF (.TIF), Wave (.WAV), Midi (.MID), Audio-visual Interface (.AVI), etc.
- Incorporating new developments in Information Technology is a norm at LibSys. It supports a wide spectrum of hardware / software platforms in Client-Server environment.
- LibSys is field-proven software with more than 800 sites in wide range of organisations. LibSys has a contract with The British Council Division to provide automation and related services for its libraries in India and South Asian countries. LibSys is already operational in 20 of their libraries.
- The Spanish version of LibSys has been installed successfully at Universidad Nacional, Heredia, Costa Rica (Central America).
- For its LibSys Network (LSNet) activities, LibSys is providing the solution of a Union Catalogue to its users. Software is currently available to link these Union catalogues on-line. These facilities of LibSys make networking of libraries effective and promote the sharing of resources.

It is a full integrated multi-user system designed to run on super micro/ mini computers (including PCs) under UNIX/XENIX/VMS environment. A subset of LIBSYS is also available for micro under MS-DOS. LIBSYS is easy to operate and the library staff can begin to use it quickly without any prerequisite programming/computer skills. It ensures high productivity because of minimal data entry requirements, maximum possible integration of functions and powerful search and query facilities. LIBSYS supports almost all activities relating to acquisition, cataloguing, circulation and serials.

Each sub-system of LIBSYS described below gives the menu followed by some details of its main processes.

Acquisition

The acquisition sub-system deals with ordering monitoring of receipts and invoice control. It also supports budget expenditure analysis.

Acquisition Menu

---

1. Initiate titles
2. Approval process
3. Update title details
4. Place order
5. Receiving

6. Accessioning
7. Payment requisitions
8. Order follow up
9. Amend cancel order
10. Renew standing order
11. Inquiries
12. Reports
13. Record keeping
14. System setup

Cataloguing

This sub-system makes available various catalogues/ indexes online for instant reference. It has a powerful data entry facility, which also provides formats (MARC) such as LCMARC, OCLC etc.

Cataloguing Menu

1. Title in-process
2. Cataloguing
3. Remove title record
4. Author catalogue
5. Update holdings
6. Title catalogue
7. Classified/ subject catalogue
8. KWIC/ KWOC index
9. Holdings summary
10. Catalogue cards
11. Keyword based searches (Boolean)
12. SDI, current awareness/bibliographies

Circulation

This sub-system maintains

(1) Up-to-date membership records
(2) The latest status of collection meant for circulation

It performs all the function related to circulation providing suitable checks at every stage. It takes care of infrequent, but routine functions such as bindery record management, display of recent additions and so on.

Circulation Menu

1. Membership records
2. Collection records
3. Issue
4. Return
5. Renewal
6. Reservation
7. Recalling
8. Inquiries
9. Report
10. System setup

Serials

This sub-system is an independent system, which provides control of periodical subscription and subsequent monitoring of the scheduled arrival of individual issues. It maintains record or budget sanctioned for serials under different categories; amount encumbered and expended thus providing complete budgetary control. This sub-system also handles serials, which may be received by exchange.

Reader Services

Users in library can search the bibliographic database and find specific information online which would not normally be possible from traditional catalogues. The search facility also tells the availability of each item for circulation, including current status of individual copies of a little.

Following catalogue are available online:

- Title catalogue
- Author catalogue
- Subject catalogue
- Classified catalogue
- KWIC/KWOC indexes

Boolean Search

The Boolean search can be made on keywords from any of the bibliographic data. The uses of the logical connectors OR AND NOT are allowed. The search facilitated by using Truncation, use of parenthesis, proximity connectors.

Specialized Services

SDI, CAS, List of recent arrivals, specific bibliographies, import of bibliographic, import and export of bibliographic data in standard exchange formats etc.

LIBSYS is developed in 'C' language. It supports its own index generation procedures. Therefore it doesn't require purchasing of any database software. However, if required, LIBSYS can be modified to operate on any preferred database such as ORACLE etc. It is being enhanced to support CD-ROM, networking (LAN and Remote) and multi-lingual use. These upgrades would be available to all the existing installations of LIBSYS.

Presently LibSys is Available as Following Two Products:

LibSys 4

A standard product with full fledged functionalities as usually required in universities, large academic institution, special libraries, public libraries, etc.

LS Ease

A downsized product derived from LibSys4 for corporates, colleges and school libraries where some special functionality may not be required. However, LSEase adequately meets the requirement of a modern growing library.

Both LibSys4 and LSEase can be implemented in Client-Server mode providing complete range of features expected from any advanced library system.

An effective workflow is provided through following integrated systems:

- Acquisition/Ordering
- Cataloguing
- Circulation
- Serials Control
- OPAC (Online Searching of Bibliographic Information)

Following 'Add on' facilities are available in the standard LibSys4 and LSEase:

LS Web OPAC

Making available OPAC is on a browser on internet or intranet.

LS Web Clent

To run the entire LibSys4/LSEase through web browser. This Applet-Servlet implementation avoids loading of any software component on client machines.

LS Mirroring

Enables maintaining a mirror image of LibSys database on other server machine. Allows working on any database and simultaneously updates both the databases.

LS Unicode

Option provides handling data in unicode thus enabling support on various languages/ scripts around the world including regional languages in India.

LSmart

For self check-out, book drop etc. in a security system installed in the library.

LibSys4

- Standard
  - Small Library (Upto 60,000 entries)
  - Special Edition (Upto 20,000 entries)
  - Single Stand Alone (Upto 60,000 entries)
- Global Edition

LS Ease

- Enterprise Edition
- Standard
  - Small libraries (Upto 30,000 entries)
  - Special (Upto 10,000 entries)
    - Single User Standalone
- College Edition
  - Multi-user Lan
  - Single User Standalone
- School Edition
  - Multi-user Lan
  - Single User Standalone

Special Features

LibSys, an Integrated Library Management Software, has following salient features:

- Client-Server model
- Various Options for Server
- Choice for Client
- Multi-lingual support for Indian and International Languages/Scripts
  - ISM Publisher (C-DAC, India)
  - GIST ((C-DAC, India)
  - User-friendly Windows GUI
  - Supports TCP/IP for Communication
- Z39.50 compliant (Both search engine and LibSys Clients)
- Co-operative Cataloguing (Network Downloading)

- Web OPAC
- MARC Implementation
  UNIMARC
  MARC21 (USMARC+CANMARC)
  UKMARC
  CCF
- Import/Export of Data in Marc and non MARC
- Supports Barcode/ Smart card/ RFID for capturing of member ID and item ID
- Supports Barcode/ Smart card/ RFID for capturing of member ID and item ID
- Interface with Digital Video Camera (to capture member's photograph)
- In-built Barcode Printing
- Optional Back-End RDBMS (ORACLE or SQL Server or MYSQL) with ODBC connectivity.
- e-mail interface
- Support Electronic Resources
- URL
- Multi-media files (TIFF, GIF, JPEG, Wave, Midi, etc.)
- PDF file
- Other file formats
- Optional Add-on features

Operating Platforms

LibSys supports open system architecture, from host multi-user system to Client-Server implementation to a total web-based solution. So there are a number of operating platforms to choose from.

Server Options

- UNIX
- LINUX
- Pentium machine with SCO Unix/Unix Ware
- SunSparc with Solaris
- Alpha with OSF/1
- RS/6000 with AIX
- HP-9000 with HP-UX
- SG with IRIX
- Windows NT/2000/XP
- Windows 95/98/NT/2000/XP (Stand Alone)

Client Options

- Standard Windows (95/98/NT/2000/XP)
- Web Enabled (Applet-Servlet implementation)
- Unix Workstations
- X-Windows Workstations (xterm)
- VT220 & compatible terminals
- Thin Java clients

RDBMS Options

LibSys doesn't need an RDBMS as it is built around its own proprietary bibliographic database. However, the option of LibSys with SQL Server, ORACLE, MySQL as back-end RDBMS with odbc interface is also available.

Support

The post sales support for installation of LibSys software and its smooth operations at a site, is provided by Customer Support Group. The CSG has a team of 25-30 professionals having good blend of knowledge and experience with operating systems, networking and library and information science. To cover sites across the country, there are four Regional Offices in New Delhi, Mumbai, Bangalore and Kolkata. There is adequate staff in the Regional Offices to provide effective and timely support to sites. The backup support is provided from the corporate office.

Installation

Prior to installation, LibSys guides user in deciding Server configuration and establishing a LAN in the library. When user confirms the availability of computing environment, Customer Support Executive visits the site to do LibSys software installation and setting up of parameters for the users. Upto 2 days on-site briefing on LibSys is provided to staff to enable them to start using LibSys.

During this phase, LibSys also takes up conversion of any existing machine-readable data (cds/isis, dBase, MARC, etc.) to LibSys database. Whenever required, programming efforts are put for effective data conversion.

Training

Besides 2 days on-site overview/training on LibSys at the time of installation, there is provision for more comprehensive training arranged at the Regional offices (or at training centers as arranged by LibSys) during the year as per the schedule released in advance.

Regular Support

Comprehensive regular support as part of warranty support or under Annual Maintenance and Development contract is available to users which include Counselling on phone, e-mail, fax, courier or through internet connectivity. Whenever need arises site visits are made by CSE as per specific requirement of the user. In a nutshell, LibSys gives special emphasis on support aspect of project implementation.

LSEase

LSEase is an offshoot of LibSys, the most popular and widely used Library software in the country. LSEase has a mixed blend of functionalities and technology that abundantly meet the automation requirements on any growing library which may not need some special functionality required in large universities, public libraries and special libraries. LSEase covers all the operations of libraries of different sizes including Web-enabled search facility. It continues to be outstanding in this market segment because of carrying over international standards such as options for MARC implementation, Client-Server architecture, facility to run on various operating systems, support on multi-media files such as images, videos, music, etc. from its parent system - LibSys.

In short, LSEase is an affordable solution having best of functions, features and technology.

Easy to operate with user-friendly worksheets, LSEase doesn't require any pre-requisite programming or computer skills, and the library staff can begin to use it quickly. LSEase, with an excellent user interface, is interactive, screen-oriented, and is menu driven. It has the facility to set user-defined security at function level. The system is not only easy-to-operate, but also can be easily implemented.

LSEase operates effectively in different environments resulting in higher productivity. The proprietary indexing features inherited from LibSys give remarkably good response time for bibliographic searches even for large databases.

LSEase covers the following modules:

- Acquisition
- Cataloguing
- Circulation
- Serials
- OPAC (Online Searching of Bibliographic Information)

LSmart Solutions

LSmart is a suite of applications harnessing RFID technology for use in libraries. It is the result of integrating efforts of LibSys software with various RFID products of France based TAGSYS (former division of GemPlus, world's number one smart card solution provider). LSmart, having Security System through EAS gates as its core component, can be implemented in phased manner enhancing operational efficiency at every stage.

Components of LSmart include:

RFID Tags/Labels

RFID smart labels are flexible paper-thin with an electronic chip. They are designed for lasting to lifetime of the item they identify. When placed into books or other media, they can be read and written to using radio frequency, which operates without contact and line of sight. They have an EAS (Electronic Article Surveillance) function to detect thefts.

Multipurpose Station

To be operated by library staff, it enables handling of books and other material having RFID Labels/Tags (also referred as Smart Labels). It provides for the following functions: -

Tagging

After sticking RFID label on the book, its information such as Accession No. is registered in the chip of the label. This function allows writing such information on chip either from the LibSys database or by scanning existing barcode label, if any.

Checking-out

After establishing the validity of a member card either by barcode reader or by smart card reader, the books to be checked-out of the library are placed on the deck of the station. The corresponding LSmart function updates the LibSys database and the theft detection system into the smart label is deactivated. All this happens automatically when staff is in the process of replacing the existing book by another book being checked-out by the same borrower. A receipt is printed out confirming details of borrowed material and due date.

Checking-in

The books returned by the borrower are put on the deck of the station. The corresponding LSmart function would calculate the late fine, if any, and would update the LibSys database. Simultaneously, the theft detection system into the smart label is automatically activated. Optionally, a receipt is also printed out to confirm returning of borrowed material. Books can be placed on deck station one by one without any intervention by staff.

Renewal

The books to be renewed are put on the deck of station. The corresponding LSmart function would check the validity of renewal and accordingly update the LibSys database. A receipt is printed out confirming renewal of book and new due date.

Smart Label Monitoring

The status of theft detection system into the smart tag/label of any book can be found out by placing the same on the deck of the station. Further, the theft detection system can either be activated or deactivated on the smart label.

Sorting

When book is put on the deck, LSmart flashes collection and shelf no. which facilitates shelving of items. While sorting the checked-in books, LSmart provides additional information such as item belonging to other location or if it is a reserved item, etc.

Admin Function

To view the status of various components installed as part of LSmart solution. It can change the status of a component or reset the state of component, etc. from remote.

Security Gate

The security gates are two or more Theft Detection Pedestals (AES) which are independent of each other and also have overlapping protection zones providing additional security. Any item that has not been checked-out either by staff station or self check-out station will be detected as it goes past these pedestals. The Theft Detection Pedestals will work even when LSmart is down as a single technology is used for item management and theft prevention.

Self Borrowing Station

This is a self-service station where the books are checked out of the library independently by the borrower without any intervention of library staff. It is an interactive station/kiosk with touch screen which prompts the patron to enter his/her library card (either bar coded or smart card as per the configuration of the station). The LSmart function checks the validity of the member card and further prompts to place the books on to the deck of the Borrowing Station. The status of each book as checked-out is automatically updated on the LibSys database. The theft detection system of the smart label for that book is de-activated to enable smooth passage from the security gate. A receipt is issued to the patron confirming details of borrowed books along with due date.

Book Drop

As books are returned through the Book Drop facility located suitability in a library, the smart labels are automatically read and LSmart will immediately update both patron record and library database. The theft detection system into the smart labels is simultaneously activated. The Book Drop allows patrons to return items 24 hours a day. Optionally, a conveyor sorting system for books that are returned through the Book Drop can be installed.

Book drops could also be in the form of remote kiosks placed at various locations in the building / premises of the institute to enable patrons to drop the book for check-in to library at their own convenience without visiting library.

Self Operating multi-purpose Station

A new kiosk design is being developed so that one station can be used for self check-out, self check-in and renewal. Such multi-purpose station could be cost effective and quite useful for small library setup.

Shelf Management

Inventory controls on shelves are rapidly and accurately performed using special handheld terminal supplied by TAGSYS. Smart labels secured in books can be read in seconds. Up to 64,000 book ID numbers can be stored in the reader memory, which is then downloaded to the central database through one of the LSmart interface. It has an audible signal to indicate successful item identification.

4.3.6 LS/2000 SOFTWARE

The integrated library system from OCLC is a microcomputer-based system that provides bibliographic file maintenance circulation control, online catalogue searching and other automated services. Serial control and acquisitions modules as well as an interactive link to OCLC's central system in Dublin, Ohio are planned.

LS/2000 is an enhanced version of the Integrated Library System (ILS) developed at Listen Hill National Centre for Biomedical Communications of the National Library of Medicine. OCLC selected ILS as the basis for LS/2000 because it is an integrated system, Compatible for MARC format, and provides flexible parameters that allow library staff to tailor the system to meet their individual library needs.

Cataloguing Subsystem

LS/2000 has many features designed for cataloguing and circulation staff, Library staff.

---

(1) Library staff can enter and edit bibliography and copy-specific cataloguing and either transmit the information from OCLS's On line union catalogue via a printer port interface or enter this information directly on LS/2000.

(2) The system provides quick cataloguing using previously stored bibliographic records for additional copies or volumes.

(3) LS/2000 has full, interactive authority control for both transfer and direct entry. Each library defines its own authority files.

(4) New and edited records are automatically checked against these authority files. Catalogue and authority review file allows supervisory personnel to review and approve the work of other staff.

(5) Both the bibliographic and authority files are compatible with the MARC format. The Library can define local fields, as it desires.

Circulation Subsystem

The Circulation Subsystem contains functions for check in and checks out, recall, review, and holds. There is also a Reserve Book room function. Special function allows staff to prepare mailing tables, change holds queue priorities, print full slips, define registration work forms, and register patrons. Circulation functions utilize bar code scanners. Library staff defines the loan, overdue, fine, review, and hold policies, as well as the calendar for days the library is closed.

Administrative & Technical Subsystems

It allows library staff to enter policy and system information to support the bibliographic, circulation and retrieval system and to design the reports and notices to be provided by the system.

The board range of parameters available with LC/2000 allows the library staff to define the bibliographic record, authority files, and indexes for their local online catalogue.

---

1. The online catalogue is integrated with the Bibliographic and circulation subsystem.
2. Bibliographic and authority records are compatible with the MARC format.

3. Flexible parameters allow the library staff to tailor the online catalogue to meet the needs of their library's staff and patrons.

Search

Users can search the online catalogue using a variety of search keys, including author, title, subject heading keyword, call number, ISSN or ISBN, and OCLC number. Library staff can select additional access points at their option searching is menu driven and allows truncation and use of the Boolean 'AND' operator. LS/2000 remember the previous screens seen during a search and provides searching controls that can be used at any time to end a search, Back up to the previous display, get brief instructions obtain help, move forward through a list. With LS/2000 libraries can structure a local catalogue system that answers the individual library's needs.

OCLC has also announced its new LS/2000 Micro series of local library systems that are designed for small libraries, specialised sub collections. It features Winchester disk technology in conjunction with either a Data Central S/120 or DC-compatible PDP series computer. Costs saving standard profiles are available for medical libraries. Depending on options selected, a system can support up to thirty terminals.

The LS/2000 Micro Series currently offers an Online Public Access Catalogue, circulation control, bibliographic and authority file maintenance, with serials control available in 1985.

4.3.7 MECSYS SOFTWARE

MECSYS is Information Management Software. It is a comprehensive and total software solution for a fully computerized technical library environment, developed by MECON, RANCHI.

It provides necessary tools for conveniently storing and rapidly retrieving information. It is competent enough to handle all the activities of a modern Technical Information Center in the areas of information storage, Information maintenance etc. Current and accurate information can be obtained immediately from different databases. MECSYS is able to deliver the speed, capacity, flexibility and ease of database loading that would enable to keep all the information up to date and instantly accessible.

It can also handle memos correspondence, reminders, reports etc. Software offers complete user friendliness and is fully menu driven. It provides different levels of security for users and the library staff. It also pinpoints actual storage of documents.

MECSYS is total information Management System, originally developed to provide comprehensive yet cost effective on line retrieval services and technology. It is a powerful efficient software package, field tested in actual Library environment for over 3 years.

Modules

Based on typical requirements of environment of a technical library, MECSYS has been modularized into subsystems as below:

1. User's information subsystem provides a wide range of assistance to users as they walk into the library. The retrospective search and information dissemination facility enables a user to search through the entire database for biographic information on different fields using Thesaurus of keywords. A user

profile can be maintained and information from the database can be distributed selectively using this profile. This module also shows new arrivals, expected arrivals, personal current status library holding statistics etc. and provides facilities like acquisition, reservation, weekly titles service, abstract service and information exchange service.

2. Circulation control facilitates online return/issue/renewal of books and reading materials providing suitable checks at each stage. This includes overdue reminders and reservations by users etc. It provides membership for enrolment of personal and institutional borrowers. Its functions include registration of a member, membership renewal and its cancellation. This module keeps track of Inter library loans and generates status reports regarding lost/missing/issued/under-binding documents for stock verification. It also displays day wise issue/return/renewal statistics.
3. Serials control for subscribed and other periodicals including monitoring of binding activities, reminders/renewals etc. Arrival status and list of articles of a periodical can be maintained. It has a system for tracking for missing issues and generation of reminders based on regular periodicity of serials taking into account feedback received from the publisher about delayed issues. This module helps in new subscription/renewal of periodical by printing new subscription request/ renewal request. Details of an invoice are also maintained with a facility for advance payment generally needed for foreign document. In case invoice is not received within stipulated time then reminder is generated automatically.
4. Requisition–to-accessioning of books, standards, handbooks etc. through 'Acquisition control module including generation of purchase orders and their status monitoring. Before processing a request system checks from database whether the said document is available in library holding or on order list. An accession no. is assigned to each document; this can be either system generated or user defined as per the setup of the installation. The moment a document is catalogued automatically and the holding are updated. This module also maintains suppliers/ publishers' profile.
5. Data entry module or subsystem provides screen based form representations facilitating entry of records including those for 'weekly Article services, 'new Arrivals' etc. Annual data book can also be maintained for information on different organizations, countries, industry population, culture etc.
6. Subsystems for overall administration like maintaining routine backup of huge database, user's administration and other resource management. Word performance reports can also be generated on different activities of the library for efficient management.

Information Retrieval

In MECSYS, any query can be made on any field in the database by giving whatever little information is known. A refined search will eliminate irrelevant records and save ones hours of needless browsing. Besides the basic mode of searching, a number of features provide added capabilities for updating/formatting, printing, sorting, routing documents to someone else's terminal or printer.

Following modes of search are incorporated:

a. on precise access points
b. right/left truncated access points
c. keyword terms
d. combination search.
  - A precise access point is any item specified in exactly the same way, as it is known to the system.
  - Right/left truncated access points are given instead of specifying a precise access point and proceeded/succeeded with asterisk mark.
  - In keyword terms searching the access points for search may be keyword like STEEL. Boolean combination of keywords is also possible.
  - COMBNIATION SEARCH: Logical 'OR' the union operator; logical 'AND' and intersection operation; logical 'NOT' the rejection operator, proximity connectors: there is one intersection operator where the two keywords are adjacent.

The software package is fully operational in the library of MECON at RANCHI.

4.3.8 SLIM (SYSTEM FOR LIBRARY INFORMATION MANAGEMENT)

SLIM library management software is a product of Algorythms Consultants Pvt. Ltd. Pune, established in 1989. The software is constantly upgraded to remain in the forefront of technological developments in the field of IT and to cater to the changing scenarios in managing libraries. SLIM++ is a 32-bit application developed on the Windows platform. This software comes in various modules and each one of them can get integrated with the other modules at any given point of time. This software comes with an unlimited multi user license.

Informatics (India) Limited, Bangalore is the authorised distributor of Algorythms, Pune in India.

SLIM++ is integrated, multi-user, multi-tasking library information software for the Windows environment.

SLIM++ helps you catalogue books, films, sound recordings, drawings, clippings, articles, reports, letters, pamphlets, serials publications... all those things that contain information so vital to your organization. SLIM++ cataloguing adheres to popular international standards. This means you can exchange data with the world. Retrieval of the data is simple, fast and efficient. Even a catchy phrase in the description of the catalogued item can be used for searching.

SLIM++ is designed and developed in modules to take care of complete functionality required for automating libraries. You can configure SLIM++ software for your library by selecting one or more of these standard and add-on modules. These modules exhibit features that make SLIM++ a top class software.

SLIM++ modules work on the same data from different nodes of a network. They can be installed independent of each other on different desktops. SLIM++ works just as well on a stand-alone machine as it does in a network of Computers. Moreover, your library can be browsed through the Internet / intranet with SLIM++.

Modules

- Cataloguing
- Circulation
- Serials Control
- Acquisition
- OPAC
- Web based OPAC
- Current Awareness Service (CAS)
- Selective Dissemination Information (SDI)
- Web proposals
- Inter Library Loan
- Statistical Analysis
- Import Export
- Z39.50 Server
- Z39.59 Client & More

General Features

Scope of SLIM++ is very exhaustive, and a lot of attention is paid to the details of library management functions in its design. At the same time, a high degree of comfort in operation of the software is achieved by incorporating the following:

On-line help /Manual	Pick-up lists during data entry
Validation checks	Bar code support
Minimal data entry	Multimedia Links
Data captured in the export / import format similar to MARC / CCF, ISO 2709	Browsing your library information through the Internet/Intranet
Multi-script with multiple fonts	Packing / purging of records
Variable length fields / records	Optimal use of disk storage
Integrity checks	Existing database conversion to SLIM++
Optional customized data entry	Optional customized data capture
Variety of selection criteria for reports. Reports can be viewed on screen printed straight-away stored in disk files	Letters user defined default texts optional editing of prepared letters sending letters through e-mail

Windows GUI Features

Adherence to Windows Standards with menu bar, taskbar, window resizing, window moving, multi-tasking using simultaneous operations in multiple windows.

Point and Click, reduces users learning requirements

Drag & Drop, Cut & Paste reduces data entry effort and thereby increases uniformity and accuracy of the data.

Wizard mode for beginners: eg. wizard mode to enter item information, to formulate search query. Users don't have to remember steps; neither can they miss out any steps.

Extensive Online Help

Tool tips

- Use of RTF (rich text format) for reporting allows user specified fonts, colours and sizes for texts.
- Double click to open files and multi-media links to sounds, films, drawings, bitmaps, web sites etc.
- Interface with standard Windows applications like WordPad, MS-Word, Mail Exchangers, Object packagers etc.
- Use of Windows standard dialogues for saving, opening and searching.

Modules Details

1. *Cataloguing*

SLIM++ Cataloguing is based on AACR2 (Anglo American Cataloguing Rules, 1988). Catalogue any type of material:

- Books ,
- Micro-documents ,
- Slides ,
- Maps,
- Audio / video cassettes ,
- Drawings ,
- Films ,
- Texts ,
- Clippings ,
- Serial publications

Descriptions of AACR2 areas / sub areas / other categories are available on-line. MARC fixed fields are provided. Data entry for a card is entirely menu driven. Rules of punctuation are programmed to give consistent and accurate cards. The cards are available in the standard 5" × 3" size. Analytical entries, 'See', 'See also' references and multiple catalogues are available. Unlimited numbers of added entries (access points) per card are allowed such as title, uniform title, multiple keywords, place of conference, etc. Any subject classification system such as UDC, DD, or CC is permissible.

Other Features

- Authority control on author/publisher name/keyword
- Accession details of items
- Cardex for bound volumes of journals
- Micro-document cataloguing (article indexing)
- Bibliographic details of serials
- Accession register
- Catalogues and labels printing

2. *Circulation*

SLIM++ Circulation system is based on lending rules that you can define and change. It covers:

- Member information/registration card
- Subjects of interest for members (SDI)
- Loans and reservations data retrieval by borrower identification
- Front desk operations
- Issues, returns, reissues
- Reservations/cancellations
- Bulk transactions for a borrower
- Backdated transaction

Other Features

- Inventory/circulation status
- Physical stock verification
- Binding (issues/receipts)

Shelf List

- Calendar master for maintaining institute/library holidays
- Deferred reservations to ensure availability of an item on shelf at a specified future date
- Transaction logging

- Rules based computation of fines for overdue items
- Tracking fines and fees due
- Prioritized reservation queues
- Inter library loan monitoring system

Calendar

- Letters generation
- Collect reserved item
- Overdue loans notice
- No dues certificate
- Membership renewal reminder
- Recall a book in circulation
- SDI (selective dissemination of information)

The Issue / Return Application

It provides an easier interface to the **barcode** system, offering basic transactions like Issue and Return. You may also print transaction report for a borrower.

3. *Serials Control*

SLIM++ serials control system helps achieve an effective utilization of periodicals budget. It allows for tracking receipts of issues, filing claims for issues not received, preparing binding orders, etc. It includes:

Journal title and related information

Publisher/agent	Periodicity
Delivery mode	Subject
Gratis/exchange	Addresses for communication
Subscription order	Subscription payment details
Issue details	
Cardex for loose issues	
Issues arrived	
Issues not received	
Missing/damaged issues	
Duplicate issues	
Issues in bindery	
Issues borrowed	Publisher details
Agent details	Journal cataloguing as per AACR2

Separate list for journals on proposals

Letters Generation

- New subscription
- Renewal of subscription
- Reminders/replacements for issues
- Binding order
- Request/acknowledgment for gift/exchange
- Payment forwarding note

Additional Facilities

- Generation of arrival schedule for issues of journal
- Subscription history for journals
- Popularity statistics
- Accessioning of bound volumes
- Publication history

4. *Acquisition*

SLIM++ Acquisition system supports the entire range of activities from the time someone makes a proposal or a recommendation to acquire an item, until it is finally paid for and accessioned. It covers:

- Proposal for acquisition
- Inquiry to book sellers/publishers
- Purchase orders (foreign/local)
- Books on approval memos
- Purchase bills
- Payment details of purchase bills
- Credit notes
- Detailed information about vendors
- Multiple currencies and conversion rates

This data is automatically picked up for generating numerous letters. These can be simply printed, signed and posted. Items on proposals may be searched using author names or titles. The items are grouped by proposes, subjects, recipients, etc. and can be retrieved in many ways:

- Those on requests, orders, bills or approval memos
- Those awaiting approval

- Those received on donation or exchange basis
- Associated payments information is maintained. Purchase follow-ups are made easy with:
- Purchase order status report
- Purchase order follow up letters
- Payment advices
- Entries in accession register are generated automatically.

Items under acquisition are also visible through OPAC browsers.

5. *OPAC (On-line Public Access Catalogue)*

SLIM++ OPAC offers powerful on-line search facilities to search through library catalogues:

Author	Keyword	Subject class
Title	Publisher	Place of publication
Main entry	Material type	Place of conference
Subject name	ISBN / ISSN	Year of conference
Series titles	Serials title	Year of publication

The repository of words, names, titles, keywords, etc. is available for on-line browsing while the search phrase is being entered. This enables display of alternate spellings, words derived from same root and helps the searcher by providing a view of the data. In addition to these conventional searching methods, OPAC indexes every word in the description of the item. Thus, to conduct a search one need not be aware of the cataloguing style of the library.

Optional formats are available to display information such as:

- Abstract of the item
- Keywords for the item
- Number of copies
- Circulation status such as:
  - current borrower
  - due date
  - reservations
- Bound volumes of a journal
- Loose issues of a journal
- Inventory status such as lost / missing / withdrawn
  - An interactive query builder with
  - Boolean operators such as *and, or, not*
  - Wild card matching
  - Proximity and adjacency operators

- Set formation and combination operators
- A query result can be presented as a neatly formatted bibliography in multiple sorting orders.
- Advantages of SLIM software over software developed In-house

In case you are wondering whether you should develop a Library software in house, we request you to consider the following points and then choose SLIM as your library software.

Ready to Use from Day One

SLIM has exhaustive set of library management functions. Hence the library gets computerised in all respect. In case of in-house developed software many functions remain in the process of development. Library staff has to work with the manual procedures as well as with the computer system. This results in doing double work for the library staff.

Cost Effective

SLIM software is developed by team of computer professionals along with library professionals and astute readers over last eight years. The cost of development runs into many man-years. It comes to you at the price of a few man-months. Developing the software in-house with all its functionality will surely exceed the cost what you are paying for SLIM.

Proven Software

SLIM is implemented at over hundred libraries. It is a stable product. In case of in-house system, the development cycle will go through many trials and errors. You are paying for the time and efforts of your library and the development staff during this time.

After Sale Support

SLIM software is supported by our team of engineers. In case of in-house software, this support may not be possible for various reasons such as

- Non availability of in house engineer- who may be pre-occupied developing other systems.
- Man-power turnover - new person who takes over the development may not know what has been done so far. Hence again starts from the beginning.
- Continuous up gradation of the software to keep pace with the latest technological advances may not be possible as maintaining library software need not be the focus area of the original development team.

6. *Web Aware OPAC*

SLIM++ on the Internet

SLIM++ has the capability of putting your library information on the WWW / INTRANET. This module allows the user to login as a library member and view his/her loans and reservations. He/She can even reserve an item in the library through the internet. Along with all these features, catalogue browsing, circulation details, word/phrase search, view card etc. are also available.

All this information appears as different web pages on the NET. The appearance of these pages can be customised by you.

Retrieval of the data is simple, fast and efficient. Even a catchy phrase in the description of the catalogued item can be used for searching.

Intranet/Internet Capabilities

On-line searching of library collection for remote user or user using heterogeneous computer terminals using the Internet/Intranet technology.

Searching other On-Line databases/sites and downloading the information into library's collection both as catalogued items and the cataloguing entries.

Following are SLIM++ based Libraries on Internet:

- National Center for Radio Astrophysics
- IUCAA
- Bioinformatics

7. *Bulletin Printing (CAS Current Awareness Service)*

SLIM++ helps in the publication of an information bulletin containing particulars of the latest additions of books or articles. The list in the bulletin is arranged in the order of subjects. The particulars of the items can include abstracts besides the standard bibliographic data and library call numbers. A Keyword or an author name index to the list is also prepared.

This report can be prepared either in the Rich Text Format or the HTML Format. The report when created in the HTML format gets automatically linked to the Web Aware OPAC module of SLIM++.

Fonts, sizes, colours, elements of bibliography and their sequence are defined by users and are placed in a persistent form. With the RTF format output, it is possible to further enhance the publication using word processors, if required.

8. *SDI (Selective Dissemination of Information Service)*

This application lets you prepare a bibliography report per library member:

This report contains the bibliography of those recently acquired library items in which the member is interested. The generated report can be printed, stored into a file or can be mailed to the borrower.

9. *WEB Proposals*

This module allows library members to propose (suggest) books for purchase using web-based suggestion forms. These forms are viewed by the library staff using acquisition module and books are either marked for approval with the name of the approving authority or approved for purchase by the staff. The approver sees the list of books meant for his/her approval on web and can mark some of the books for purchase.

Web Proposals Covers:

- View Proposals List.
- Propose an Item online.
- View the list of Proposals proposed only by the member.
- View List of items for approval if the member is an approver.

10. *Statistical Analysis*

This Module produces different statistical information required for library management such as

- Distribution of transactions over working-hours, week-days, or months
- Distribution of loans and overdue loans for a borrower category
- Distribution of loans and overdue loans for a subject group
- Reservation queue sizes and average waiting period

Hardware Configuration

1. Intel Pentium 333 MHz (PCI/ISA BUS) onwards128 MB RAM 1.2 GB HDD1.44 MB FDD256 KB Cache104/101 TVSE KEYBOARD2 Serial and 1 Parallel Port14" SVGA colour Monitor with 64 Bit Controller CardEthernet Card with Boot ROM (Optional if stand alone machine)
2. IOMEGA ZIP 2.2 GB/CD writer for BACKUP - Optional
3. MAIN SERVER (Required if Network is to be maintained) Intel Pentium based server @ 333 MHz onwards 128 MB EDO SIMM RAM 16 KB on-chip cache PCI/ ISA BUS256 KB High Performance write Back Second Level cache 1 × 1.44 MB Sony Floppy Disk Drive 6.00 GB SEAGATE Fast SCSI 11 Hard disk DrivePCI FAST SCSI 11 Controller capable of 10 MB/s; (Bus logic/infocom)PCI SVGA Controller2 Serial Port; 1 High speed Parallel Port; 1 Mouse Port and 1 Keyboard Port14" SVGA Colour Monitor with 64 bit PCI VGA Controller Card with 1 MB DRAM101/104 Keys TVSE KeyboardEthernet Combo Card
4. 1 × 132 Col. 24 pin DOT Matrix Printer (Optional)
5. 1 KVA Smart UPS-APC SUS 3 G UPS with 30 minutes back up timePower Chute Software for auto-shut down
6. 24 Port UTP Hub
7. Cat 5 Cabling.. + Connector Per Nodes

System software requirement:-

- Windows 9x/Windows 2000 on all nodes OR Windows NT Network C_DAC ISM software for Multi script database Personal Web Server or Windows NT IIS with option pack 4.0 installed OR Windows 2000 as server for WEB_OPAC

4.3.9 WILISYS SOFTWARE

WILISYS is a software package for Library computerization. The WIPRO information system (WILISYS) is a family of comprehensive software for library computerization. It consists of two major components:

WILIMAX	WIPRO library management system:
WILITRAX	WIPRO library abstracts system (bibliographic search)

4.3.9.1 WILIMAX library management system

This package is aimed at computerization of different activities such as house keeping operation, information retrieval etc. concerning books and periodicals.

The package can be divided into following five modules depending on the functions they perform-

(1) Acquisition:
(2) Circulation:
(3) Maintenance:
(4) Search and query:
(5) Periodicals:

1. *Acquisition*

This is a process of acquiring books for the library on request from the member. This activity can be divided into the following set of functions:

(a) Request logging
(b) Request processing
(c) Vendor selections
(d) Order placing
(e) Order monitoring
(f) Accessioning
(g) Vendor performance rating

2. *Circulation*

Activities that come under this module are

(a) New membership
(b) Charging of books
(c) Discharging of books
(d) Provision of information for items on loan its due date, reservation if any etc.
(e) Identification of items as loan to particular borrower or a class of borrowers

(f) Renewals
(g) Due date monitoring and printing reminders for over due items
(h) Fine collections and printing fines/notices
(i) Circulation Statistic
(j) Provision for handling special category of users
(k) Provision for automatic generation of due date slips and order letter for lost books

3. *Maintenance*

This module is typical information management service function. Facilities for stock checking are provided. The sub-modules of this module are:

(a) Book binding: This subsystem keeps track of a book, which has gone for binding. In addition, the binding status of book can be known.
(b) Stock checking: This helps in noting down the missing books and retain the information of these books for later use.
(c) Cataloguing: Various reports about the statistics of the library can be obtained in this module.

4. *Search and Query*

In this module, an equerry can be made on any field in the database. Any information can be held in detail by giving whatever little information is known. For instance if a person knows the title of a book he can get other details like author[s] of the book, number of copies, publisher, subject etc. this module incorporates four types of search:

- Precise access points
- Right/left truncated access points
- Keyword terms
- Combination search.

5. *Periodical Section*

This module can be viewed as a 'miniature version' of the total system. It does all the functions explained till now. In addition, it monitors the arrival of various periodicals. The functions are:

(a) Periodical ordering
(b) Periodical monitoring
(c) Periodical circulation
(d) Cancellation and replacement of periodical
(e) Periodicals maintenance.

The package is developed in "C" language using UNIFY RDBMS for data storage. A conscious effort has been made to make the design flexible enough to accommodate any changes. A judicious combination of fixed and variable length field has been made for optimum utilization of the available resources and speedy response.

II. WILITRAX Library Abstracts System

THE PACKAGE is meant for storing and retrieving abstracts information. The package is written in "C" language using UNIFY RDBMS for data storage. A conscious effort has been made to make the design flexible enough to accommodate any changes. A judicious combination of fixed and variable length field has been made for optimum utilization of the available resources and a speedy response.

Functions

Different activities covered by WILITRAX are:

- Exchange of information (abstracts) with different sources and databases,
- Maintenance of user profile,
- Dissemination of information in accordance with the user profile,
- Search of keywords in the abstract,
- Providing an interface for retrospective search on the database,
- Printing various reports and catalogues in the desired format.

These activities are grouped under the following headings:

- Information exchange,
- Selective dissemination of information (SDI),
- Retrospective search, and
- Report generation.

Information Exchange

This module enables a user to update or make a copy of the database where this system is being used. The different features of this module are:

(a) Input into the database can be made in the form of abstract data by floppy disk, cartridge or direct data entry,

(b) Standard for information exchange is International Standard 1802709.

SDI

This module maintains a user profile and disseminates the information. This process is done automatically when a new data is added on to the database.

Retrospective Search

This module enables a user to search through the database for specific abstract or information about them, based on different fields such as title, author(s), journals, year of publication, key words etc. The details are identical to those described in 'Search and Query' under 'Books' of 'WILIMAX'.

Report Generation

This module prints reports and catalogues. Salient features on this module are:

(a) Specific data for reports can be selected from the database using the 'Retrospective search' portion of the package.
(b) Reports can be printed in any desired format.
(c) Data can be sorted in any desired format.

Security Features

Security being an important feature of any system, WILISYS also provides different levels of security for users and the library staff e.g. Password.

Hardware Configuration

WILISYS has been developed in portable 'C' language. It uses UNIFY RDBMS for data management. WILISYS is implemented on WIPRO group of microcomputers under XENIX or UNIX operating system.

4.3.10 SOUL: SOFTWARE FOR UNIVERSITY LIBRARIES

SOUL is the state-of-the-art library automation software designed and developed by the INFLIBNET. It is user-friendly software developed to work under client-server environment. Although looking at the name of the software, one may think that it is meant for university libraries only, but in fact it is flexible enough to be used for automating any type or size of library.

INFLIBNET: A Gateway to India's Academic and Research Community

Information and Library Network (INFLIBNET) Centre is an Autonomous Inter-University Centre (IUC) of University Grants Commission (UGC) involved in creating infrastructure for sharing of library and information resources and services among Academic and Research Institutions. INFLIBNET works collaboratively with Indian university libraries to shape the future of the academic libraries in the evolving information environment.

SOUL - General Features

University libraries are complex entities, having large collections and serving a huge clientele. To carry out various operations in a library effectively, there is a need for automation. Computer and communication Technologies have brought revolutionary changes in the information acquisition, processing, storage, retrieval and dissemination.

Keeping in view the latest trends in Information Technology (IT), INFLIBNET Center has developed a Windows based Library Management Software "SOUL", which provides total solution for Library Automation. SOUL is designed using Client-Server Architecture which imparts extra strength to storage capacity, multiple access to single database, various levels of security, back up and storage facilities etc. This software has been designed after a comprehensive study of different library related functions practiced in university libraries. It has MS-SQL Server 7.0 or higher as the back end. This user friendly software is quite easy to work with. SOUL handles Indian languages/scripts using ISM Publisher of C-DAC. There is an effort is going on to develop a new version of software based on MARC 21 and Unicode standards and RFID protocols for electronic surveillance. The software comprises following modules:

1. Acquisition
2. Catalogue
3. Circulation
4. OPAC
5. Serial Control
6. Administration

The in-built network feature of the software will allow multiple libraries of the same university to function together as well as access to the distributed databases installed at various university libraries and union catalogue mounted at INFLIBNET using VSAT network.

1. *Acquisition*

The Acquisition module enables library staff to handle the following major functions related to acquisition of library material.

- Suggestions management.
- Ordering, cancellation and reminders.
- Receiving.
- Payment including fund control.
- Master file management such as currency, budget, vendors, publishers etc.

Through this module library staff can search the entire database of library holdings for the purpose of duplicate checking etc. Using various combinations, number of reports could be generated.

2. *Catalogue*

This module is used for retrospective conversion of books, technical processing of books received from Acquisition Section, printing a range of records for verification, searching by title and accession numbers, authority files for publishers etc. One of the unique features of SOUL is accessing to authority files on screen as well as selection box in various fields of records. Once the proposed VSAT Network by INFLIBNET is commissioned this module then will take care of automatic replication of data into union catalogue. This will avoid exchange of library data on physical media i.e. floppy, tape etc. This module covers following functions:

- Cataloguing process.
- Catalogue search.
- User services.
- Catalogue card generation.
- Authority files maintenance.
- Retro conversion.
- Stock verification.
- Report generation.
- Union database maintenance (local level).
- Export/Import of records.

3. *Circulation*

This module will take care of all possible functions deal in a university library setup. Starting from membership management, maintenance of status of library items can be handled using SOUL. The circulation transactions viz. issue, return, renewal, reserve, recall, hold can be successfully done. The complex functions like fine management for each category of user and material-wise can also be effectively managed. Inter library loan, searching the status of every member or library item is possible. Reminders for overdue material, generation of various reports have also been covered.

- Membership
- Transaction
- Inter-Library Loan
- Over due Charges
- Reminder
- Search Status
- Report Generation
- Maintenance - Lost, Binding, Damaged, Missing, Withdrawal, Reports

4. *On-line Public Access Catalogue (OPAC)*

The On-line Public Access Catalogue (OPAC) of SOUL is a window to the library collection. Using the user friendly menus, user can search for an item available in the library by author, title, corporate author, conference name, subject descriptors, class number etc. The Boolean search enables the user to conduct the search using all combinations including type of material, language, year etc. Besides, this will serve as first point of information about the library and also gateway for accessing INTERNET, union databases, or any other external sources. Web OPAC facility is also there:

- Books/Theses
- Serials
- Member Status
- Other Resources
- INFLIBNET Access

5. *Serial Control*

The complex job of keeping track of serials can easily and effectively be handled using SOUL through its Serial Control module. This module broadly handles following functions:

- Suggestions.
- Subscription (renewal and new subscription).
- Payment including fund control etc.
- Check in of issues including prediction of issues arrival.
- Reminder generation.
- Binding management.
- Search status of every item.
- Master database management.
- Reports generation etc.

6. *Administration*

User administration facility in this module is used for creating new users and giving them right for accessing different modules.

- Benefits of using SOUL.
- Available at nominal cost to university libraries.
- Software designed and developed exclusively to work under university environment.
- Network feature of the software will allow multiple libraries of university to function together.
- Exhaustive training at INFLIBNET supported by comprehensive manual.
- On-site training.
- Free updation/modification.

- Free technical assistance.
- Follows INFLIBNET's recommended standards and formats such as CCF, MARC 21, AACR2, LCSH.

System Requirement

Hardware configuration for a library to introduce SOUL software

1. *Network Version*

The software can work with minimum hardware and software configuration given below, however higher or latest configuration may be purchased to have efficiency of the software.

System for Server:

- Pentium @933 MHz with 128 MB RAM
- 40 GB HDD
- 48 x CD-ROM Drive
- 1.44" MB Floppy Drive
- Colour Monitor (SVGA)
- Ethernet card 10/100 Mbps
- Windows-NT/Windows 2000 server (Operating System)
- MS-SQL Server 7.0/Advance server 2000 (RDBMS)
- Personal Web Server or Windows NT IIS with option pack 4.0 installed OR Windows 2000 as server for Web OPAC.

System for Client:

- Pentium @933 MHz with 64 MB RAM
- 2GB HDD with 10 MB Free space
- 1.44" MB Floppy Drive
- Colour Monitor (SVGA)
- Ethernet card 10 / 100 Mbps
- Windows-95/ 98/ 2000/ XP/ NT (Operating System)

2. *College Version*

System for Server/Client:

- Pentium @933 MHz with 128 MB RAM
- 20 GB HDD with 200 MB Free space
- 48 × CD-ROM Drive
- 1.44" Floppy Drive
- Colour Monitor (SVGA)

- Ethernet card 10/100 Mbps
- Windows-98 /ME /NT / 2000 / XP / 2003 (Operating System)
- Standards supported by SOUL Software

SOUL is state of the art library management software widely used across India and neighbouring countries. SOUL adheres to internationally acceptable standards like AACR 2, CCF, MARC 21 and ISO 2709. Adoption of Standards in SOUL makes user's database globally acceptable and interchangeable.

1. *Anglo-American Cataloguing Rules-2 (AACR - 2)*

The Anglo-American Cataloguing Rules (current edition is AACR-2) are designed for use in the construction of catalogues and other lists in general libraries of all sizes. The rules cover the description of, and the provision of access points for, all library materials commonly collected at the present time. Part I deals with the provision of information describing the item being catalogued, and Part II deals with the determination and establishment of headings (access points) under which the descriptive information is to be presented to catalogue users, and with the making of references to those headings. In both parts the rules proceed from the general to the specific. AACR is co-published by the American Library Association, the Canadian Library Association, and the Chartered Institute of Library and Information Professionals (UK).

2. *Common Communication Format (CCF)*

The Common Communication Format (CCF) was developed under the auspices of United Nations Educational, Scientific and Cultural Organization (UNESCO) in order to facilitate the exchange of bibliographic data between organizations. These had begun in earnest with the project known as UNISIST (Refers to UNESCO's Intergovernmental Programme for Cooperation in Scientific and Technological Information) which involved cooperation between UNESCO and ICSU-AB (the International Council of Scientific Unions Abstracting Board).The first edition of the format was published in 1984, second edition was published in 1988 and third edition was published in 1992. It has been developed as an ISO-2709 exchange format and has adapted the second revised edition of the Anglo-American Cataloguing Rules (AACR) as a standard for data entering.

3. *MARC 21(Machine Readable Catalogue)*

MARC 21 formats are standards for the representation and communication of bibliographic and related information in machine-readable form. The MARC 21 formats are maintained by the Library of Congress in consultation with various user communities. The British Library has decided that MARC 21 will be the standard for data creation and processing of its bibliographic records. The implementation of MARC 21 by the British Library is now currently anticipated to be in the early part of 2004.

4. *ISO 2709*

The ISO 2709 computer format is the universal standard which is used in the library world for bibliographic records. ISO 2709 is a content-independent specification of fielded text for data exchange. Its primary advantage is that it is widely used by libraries, archives and visual resource collections worldwide. A large market of commercial software has developed capabilities to import and export data in this form. A secondary advantage is that the record structure is simple for humans to understand.

General Conditions

1. Taxes will be extra as applicable, presently Nil.
2. A free training on installation and operation of SOUL software will be conducted at INFLIBNET Centre, Ahmedabad. Dates will be conveyed in advance. Library may depute a professional for this training programme.
3. No TA/DA will be paid by INFLIBNET Centre for attending the training programme at INFLIBNET Centre, Ahmedabad.
4. The above software is warranted for a period of one year from the date of supply.
5. Payment should be made by way of Demand Draft drawn on any Nationalized Bank, in favour of Director, INFLIBNET Centre, payable at Ahmedabad. Payment should be made immediately after the completion of training at INFLIBNET Centre, Ahmedabad. The SOUL Software along with accessories will be handed over to the person.
6. If, above rate, terms and conditions are acceptable to you, please send your confirmed purchased order to the Director, INFLIBNET Centre, Ahmedabad to proceed further.
7. We reserve the right to accept or reject any order fully or partly without assigning any reason thereof.
8. If your university has purchased first copy and if the order is placed through them, then your college is eligible for option Sr. No. 2.

Training Programme

The Center organise a five days intensive training programme for those who have purchased the SOUL software or already sent the purchase order for procuring the software. During this training programme all the modules of the SOUL software will be taught with adequate hands on experience with computers. The centre has a well equipped laboratory with P4 systems and peer to peer network facility. Each participant will be provided a system to have hands on experience of the software. The theory and practical sessions are handled by trained faculty members of INFLIBNET.

The Centre also conducts onsite SOUL training programme called IRTPLA (INFLIBNET Regional Training Programme in Library Automation) in Universities situated in different parts of the country to give awareness to the Library professionals for automating their Libraries.

After completion of the training programme, if SOUL users face any kind of problems in using the software they should feel free to contact INFLIBNET. The concerned staff will help to solve their queries. Queries can me made through email, telephone or any other mode of communication to the SOUL software support staff at any time.

Benefits of using SOUL

- Available at nominal cost to university libraries.
- Software designed and developed exclusively to work under university environment.
- Network feature of the software will allow multiple libraries of university to function together.
- Exhaustive training at INFLIBNET supported by comprehensive manual.
- On-site training.
- Free updation/modification.
- Free technical assistance.

Follows INFLIBNETs recommended standards and formats such as CCF, AACR2, LCSH.

4.4 EVALUATION POINTS

Library Management Software packages have become an indispensable necessity of information world. Readymade package available in the market have maximum efforts as well as time otherwise wasted in their designing. Moreover, this loads to uniformity and consistency of the procedural aspects of systems adopting them. Among all the packages available, there is not a single one, which could be labelled as the "best" because each package is designed to meet different requirements. As has already been mentioned in the previous chapters, that there are three broad categories of software packages as far as their application to library and information center is concerned: on the basis of the type of function and services to us designed to perform, namely and those performing all these functions collectively, the integrated system.

The strategies for the choice of software and from person to person, but mainly a standardized list of key factors can be determined for the evaluation of these packages. In fact, evaluation of software packages does not mean evaluation merely for bringing out the merits and demerits of the package but evaluation in terms of certain factors so to see what purpose it is going to serve in the relevant system and whether and to what degree it is suitable to serve the particular system. Here a list of the key factors to consider in examining software and choosing one applications package from another are rehearsed in general terms, clearly, there are also specific factors that must be considered in choosing any specific kind of package e.g. library management system.

4.4.1 GENERAL FEATURES

There are a number of general features of any software package to be considered and taken into account.

1. *Other People's Experience*

A well tested package that is established in a market place and with which several applications similar to that being considered are in evidence and can be examined, is generally to be preferred such a package is less likely to have buggs and should have adequate support. Other people's experiences are helpful in indicating the potential and problems of a software package and others may offer help and advice in tailoring and implementing the package.

2. *Cost*

Clearly, cost is a primary consideration in the purchase of any software package, obviously, more expensive packages offer a wider range of features and facilities, but the application under consideration may only merit a more limited expenditure. Comparisons of price of packages must be made. These may be made difficult by the fact that some software is sold separately, whilst other software is sold as part of a turnkey package which also includes hardware. Also, it is important to recognize that the price of package is only a small element in the overall cost of installing a system. In addition to hardware Cost, there will be database creation and system installation and implementation costs that will probably significantly outstrip the price of the package.

3. *Originator*

The reputation of the systems house responsible for writing software package is important to originator may be useful in assessing a new package. Some software houses are well established and have long established packages in the market place, whereas others are less stable. An established software house is more likely to be able to offer continuing support.

4. *Supplier*

Sometimes the supplier is the same as the originator, but especially with business software for microcomputers, the supplier may be an agent. Agencies may specialize in certain types of Software and /or may be selling complete systems. Obviously the supplier is an intermediary between the user and the originator and may hinder direct communication between user and originator, although the better suppliers and originators will have worked out their respective responsibilities so that the customer is offered satisfactory support.

4.4.2 TECHNICAL FEATURES

In addition to general point, there are number of technical features of software packages that it is necessary to ascertain, both when choosing between package and also in assessing whether any specific package is suitable for a given application.

1. *Language*

The programming language in which the software is written may be a high level language or assembler or, a combination of both, it is important that the language used permit the application to be run efficiently.

2. *Operating System*

The package must be suitable for running under an operating system that will run on the hardware being used.

3. *Hardware*

The software needs to be available in a version that will run on the hardware available. Alternatively, if software is being chosen before hardware, it may, nevertheless, be important to choose software that will run on a machine for which a lot of other software is available, so that additional software can be selected at a later date.

4. *Ease of Use*

Ease of use of software is clearly important. Many of the factors that might be considered are related to the quality of the man-machine interface. Factors to be considered include dialogue design (e.g. menus or commands), and screen display design. Clearly, support in the form of documentation, will influence ease of use.

4.4.3 SUPPLIED FORMAT

The supplied format may be particularly important for microcomputer system. Software, therefore, must be supplied on disks or tapes that can be run on the system and, if necessary, transferred to another medium such as hard disk.

4.4.4 SUPPORT

Support in the use of software is important if the user is to exploit the feature of the software to its utmost. In general, more support should be expected with more expensive package where the task of implementation is likely to be more daunting.

Thus, there is a significant difference in style and quantity of documentation required with, say, a simple one-function microcomputer system and a multi-function, multi-user mainframe system, documentation is, nevertheless, important in all such circumstances, support may take various forms.

1. Documentation

It includes both printed documentation and on-line help system. Any reasonable system should have both different kinds of documentation should be available, different kinds of users. At the very least, documentation should include introductory exploration of basic features, a full account of all features, a list of commands, and an on-line help system. Additional tutorial support may also be available, either on disk or in printed form.

2. Advice in Setting Up

In addition to tutorial support, some assistance in implementation a software package is to be expected. With larger systems, in particular, the contract for the purchase of the software will include a number of hours' assistance from suppliers, in order to help establish databases, input forms, report forms, and other activities.

3. Training

It may be available from the system supplier or from training centers licensed by the system supplier. Other agencies, such as educational establishments may also offer some introductory training in the use of some packages. With larger systems most suppliers will offer both on-site and off-site training. Both types of training may be suitable for different groups of staff.

4. Maintenance

Maintenance of a software package involves two areas of activity- removing any bugs or errors that might become evident in the software as it is used for a variety of applications; and improving the software so that it incorporates new facilities and concepts as fashions and requirements change. Both types of maintenance are important. Many of the established software suppliers offer maintenance contracts at around 10% of the cost of the original package. Minor upgrades are made available to users with maintenance contracts. Substantial changes to software, new versions and new modules will often be made available to existing users at preferential rates.

5. User Clubs

Many of the larger and some smaller well established software packages have user clubs or user groups, which assist in the use of software. User clubs are groups of users of software packages that have two main functions to share expertise and experience in the application of the package between different users and to discuss and present a concerted front to software suppliers concerning problems and desirable improvements and developments.

4.4.5 SOFTWARE DIRECTORIES

Software directories allow available packages to be located but they as yet provide little help in the evaluation of these packages. The information provided in these directories lack critical and evaluative information but it is also true that software evaluation is dependent on individual situations. A single microcomputer software package cannot better as the "best" for every library's in-house database system. However some general guidelines for software evaluation are applicable to every in-house database. The literature on evaluation of software for library application is still sparse, unlike the extensive literature on educational software evaluation. Library and general computing literature does contain enough information to allow for evaluation of guidelines, however, in many cases these guidelines are not unique to micro computer software selection. Many general principles of selection of automated system or software evaluation for libraries are applicable to evaluation of software for microcomputer-based databases.

The first step in any software evaluation should be the analysis of needs preparation of general specifications.

In fact it is worth considerable that how far a software package is able to fulfil the need of an organization. These needs may be multidimensional. When the needs assessment is completed and preliminary specifications have been written, it is time to evaluate how individual software packages meet these needs. Suggested evaluation strategy varies in the literature from an extremely simple to an involved process. Because the requirements of software for in-house databases are complex, the prices are usually higher than other microcomputer software and because so much staff time is involved in implementing a database system, the evaluation of software should not be overly simplified.

Tenopir advises formalizing the evaluation process by using some sort of check list to score consistency with the weighted scoring technique. Major areas that should be examined and rated in the evaluation include:

1. Vendor or producer
2. Software constraints and flexibility
3. Query language
4. Security
5. Output capabilities
6. Input capabilities and procedures
7. Documentation
8. Training
9. Hardware constraints
10. Cost

Therefore, it is evident now that the factors to be considered for evaluation may differ in accordance with the need of the environment where the actual installation has to be done.

APPENDIX A*

LIBRARY MANAGEMENT SOFTWARES AVAILABLE IN INDIA – RANGE & ORIGIN WISE

Origin	*Application Domain*		
	Large System	*Medium Range System*	*Small System*
LMSs of foreign origin	Alice for WINDOWS (OASIS) BASISplus & TECHLIBplus, TLMS	NA	NA
LMSs developed over LMS of foreign origin	DELSIS (Over BASISplus)	SANJAY (Over CDS/ISIS)	TRISHNA (Over CDS/ISIS)
LMSs of Indian origin	• LIBSYS • MAITRAYEE • MECSYS • SOUL • SUCHIKA • TULIPS • ULYSIS • WILISYS	• DLMS • GRANTHALAYA • Krvger Library • Manager; • LIBRA • LIBRARIAN • LISTPLUS • NILIS • NIRMALS	• ARCHIVES • CATMAN • GOLDEN LIBRA • LIBMAN • LIBRARY MANAGEMENT • LIBRARY MANAGER; • LIBRIS • LIBSOFT • LOAN-SOFT • SALIM; SLiM

APPENDIX B*

LIBRARY MANAGEMENT SOFTWARES AVAILABLE IN INDIA

S. No.	*LMS*	*Software Developing Group*	*Availability Status*	*Marketing & Distribution Agent in India*
1.	Alice for Windows	Softlink International, Australia	C	Softlink Asia Pvt. Ltd.,New Delhi
2.	Archives (1,2,3)	Microfax Electronic Systems, Mumbai	C	Direct
3.	BASIS plus and TECHLIB plus	Information Dimension Inc., USA	C	National Informatics Centre, New Delhi
4.	CATMAN	INSDOC, New Delhi	C	Direct
5.	DLMS(Defence Library Management System)	DESIDOC, New Delhi	F	Direct
6.	DELSIS	DELNET Society, New Delhi	C	Direct
7.	Golden Libra	Golden Age Software Technologies , Mumbai	C	Direct
8.	GRANTHALAYA	INSDOC, New Delhi	C	Direct
9.	Krvger Library Manager	Blitz Audio Visuals, Pune	C	Direct
10.	Libman	Datapro Consultency Service, Pune	C	Direct
11.	Libra	Ivy Systems Ltd., New Delhi	C	Direct
12.	Librarian	Soft-Aid, Pune	C	Direct
13.	Library Management	Raychan Sysmatics, Bangalore	C	Direct
14.	Library Manager	System Data Control Pvt. Ltd., Mumbai	C	Direct
15.	Libris	Frontier Information Technology	C	Direct
16.	Lib Soft	ET & T Corp., New Delhi	C	Direct
17.	LIBSYS	Softlink Asia Pvt. Ltd., New Delhi	C	Direct
18.	ListPlus	Computer Systems, Bangalore	C	Direct
19.	Loan Soft	Computek Computer Systems, Hyderabad	C	Direct
20.	Maitrayee	CMC Kolkata in collaboration with CALIBNET	NA	NA

(Contd.)

21.	MECSYS	MECON, Ranchi	C	Direct
22.	NILIS	Asmita Consultants, Mumbai	C	Direct
23.	Nirmals	Nirmal Institute of Computer	C	Direct
24.	Salim	Expertise, Tiruchirapalli Uptron India Ltd., New Delhi	C	Direct
25.	SANJAY	DESIDOC in collaboration with NISSAT	F	Direct
26.	Slim	Algorythms, Mumbai	C	Direct
27.	SOUL	INFLIBNET	C	Direct
28.	SUCHIKA	Direct	M	Direct
29.	TRISHNA	NISTADS, New Delhi in collaboration with NISSAT	F	Direct
30.	TLMS	TRANCE Group, Germany	C	OPAC Infosys Pvt. Ltd.,Pune
31.	TULIPS	Tata Unisys Ltd., Mumbai	C	Direct
32.	ULYSIS	WIPRO Information Technology Ltd., Secunderabad	C	Direct
33.	WILISYS	Wipro India, Bangalore	C	Direct

(C: Commercially available; F: Free against registration; M: Moderately priced; NA: Not available commercially)

APPENDIX C*

HARDWARE AND SOFTWARE REQUIREMENTS AND INTRINSIC FEATURES OF SELECTED LIBRARY MANAGEMENT SOFTWARES

S. No.	*LIBRARY MANAGEMENT SOFTWARE*	*INTRINSIC FEATURES*		*SOFTWARE & HARDWARE REQUIREMENTS*	
		Programming Language(s)	*Data Storage Techniques*	*Software Requirement*	*Minimum Hardware Requirement*
1.	Alice for Windows	C++	Relational Model	WIN 95/98	• Pentium I Processor • 32 MB RAM • 2.1 GB HD • SVGA (640 X 480 X 256) • CDROM Drive (48X) • Sound Card
2.	BASISplus TECHLIB plus DELSIS	Visual Basic	Relational Model	Server UNIX SVR 4.0 or UNIXWARE Client WIN 3.11 or above TCP/IP & PC-NFS for network and shared file services)	Server • Pentium II • 16 MB RAM • 170 MB HD • 150 MB Cartridge Client • Intel 80386 • 4 MB RAM (8 MB recommended) • 20 MB HD
3.	GRANTHALAYA	4 GL/FoxPro	Relational Model	MS DOS Ver. 6.0 & above SCO UNIX Ver. 5.32	PC-AT 486MB RAM540 MB HD
4.	LIBSYS	C, Java	B-Tree and Inverted File	Server WIN NT/ SCO UNIX/ LINUX/ UNIXWARENovell ClientWIN 95/98/NT Or X-Windows	Server • Pentium II • 16 MB RAM • 640MB HDClient • PC-AT 486 • 8 MB RAM

(Contd.)

5.	SANJAYTRISHNA	PASCAL (CDS/ISIS)	Inverted File	MS DOS Ver 3.0 & aboveCDS/ISIS Ver. 2.3 & above	PC-AT640 KB RAM 540 MB HDGIST Card (for TRISHNA)
6.	SOUL	Java	Relational Model	ServerWIN NTMSSQL Server (6.5)Client WIN 95	Server • Pentium II • 64 MB RAM • 1.2 GB HD • 32 × CDROM Drive • Ethernet Card (10/100 MBPS) Client • Pentium I • 32 MB RAM • 1.2 GB HD • Ethernet Card (10/ 100 MBPS)
7.	SUCHIKA	C++	B-Tree	MS DOS 6.0 or higher Or UNIX depending on the version of the pakage	• PC-AT 486 • MB RAM • 540 MB HD
8.	TLMS	C++, Java	Relational Model	Server WIN NT Client WIN 98	Server • Pentium III • 64 MB RAM • 6 GB HD • Client • Multimedia Kit & • CDROM Drive • Pentium Celeron • 32 MB RAM • 4 GB HD • Multimedia Kit & • CDROM Drive

* *Source*: Progress of Library Management Softwares: An Indian Scenario by *P. S. Mukhopadhyay*, (*https:*//drtc.isibang.ac.in/bitstream/1849/189/2/lmss2a.PDF)

Note: We are very much grateful to the following web sources, because we have taken a great help from them in the upgradation and collection of the software packages, production and re-production of information in this chapter. The asterisks marked chapters have been cited from the websites given below.

Websites: infolibrarian.com, informindia.co.in, libraryworld.net, info.com/librarySoftware, library.geac.com, librarysoftwares.net, web.inflibnet.ac.in. mcitconsortium.nic.in, oclc.com, multiplayergames.in

---

- About CDS/ISIS (WEBLIS) Software: www.unesco.org
- About DELMARC/ DELPLUS Software: delnet.nic.in
- About Granthalaya Software: egranthalaya.kar.nic.in
- About LibSys Software: Libsys.co.in
- About LS/2000 Software: oclc.com
- About MECSYS Software: drtc.isibang.ac.in
- About SLIM Software: Slimpp.com
- About WILISYS Software: drtc.isibang.ac.in
- About SOUL Software: web.inflibnet.ac.in

REFERENCES

1. Chowdhury, GG and Chowdhury, S – Text Retrieval and Library Management Softwares in India, NISSAT Newsletter 13,3; 1994, p.13-18.
2. Devrajan, GD and Rahelamma, AV – Library Computerization in India, New Delhi: Ess Ess Publications, 1990.
3. Harbour, RT – Managing Library Automation. London, ASLIB, 1994.
4. Haung, Samuel, T – Modern Library Technology and Reference Services, New York: Haworth Press, 1993.
5. Lancaster, FW and Fayer, EG – Information Retrieval Online, California: Melville Publishing Co., 1990.
6. LibSys Promotion Brochure, New Delhi: LibSys Inc. 2005.
7. Mukhopadhyay, PS – Progress of Library Management Softwares: An Indian Scenario.
8. Nair, R, Raman – Computer Application to Library and Information Services, New Delhi: Ess Ess Publications, 1992.
9. Rowley, J – The Electronic Library, ed. 4, London: Library Association, 1998, 316-319.
10. Satyanarayan, NR – Manual of Library Automation and Networking, Lucknow: Royal Book Agency, 2004.
11. Saxena, SC and Srivastava, RK – Evaluation of Library Software Packages Available in India, DESIDOC Bulletin of Information Technology, 18, 5, 1998.
12. Sharma, Pandey, SK – Library Computerization :Theory and Practice, New Delhi, Ess Ess Publication, 1993.
13. SOUL – INFLIBNET Newsletter 5, 2 ;1999; 1,2.
14. Summit, RK – Dialog System in Encyclopedia of Library and Information Science,V.7, New York Marcel Dekker,161-96, op. Cit. 2:31-3 2.
15. UNESCO – General Information Program and UNISIST. Teaching Package on the Use of Information Handling Standards: Computer Aspects of Bibliographic Records; Computer Hardware, Software, Paris: UNESCO, 1986.

16. UNESCO – Office of Information Programme and Services, Software Development and Applications, Division of Mini Micro CDS/ISIS Reference Manual, Paris: UNESCO, 1989.
17. Vyasmoorthy, P – Software Packages in India for Library and Information Work in Sharma, CD and Ojha DC ed. – Advances in Library and Information Science, V.3, Jodhpur: Scientific Publishers, 1992.
18. Yates, R – Library Automation: The Way Forward, Program Material 30,3; 1996.

CHAPTER 5

NETWORKS AND NETWORKING

A network consists of two or more computers that are linked in order to share resources such as printers and CD-ROMs, exchange files, or allow electronic communications etc. The computers on a network may be linked through cables, telephone lines, radio waves, satellites or infrared light beams. A typical definition of a data network today would read as : a data network is an interconnected system of computers, peripherals and software over which data, files and messages are sent and received. A more technical definition would be that a devices or nodes that can communicate with each other. The nodes may be computers, terminals, workstations or communication units or various kinds distributed over different locations. They communicate over communication channels that can be leased from common carriers (e.g. telephone companies) or are provided by the owners of the network. These channels may use a variety of transmission media, including optical fibers, coaxial cable, twisted copper pairs, satellite links or digital microwave radio signals.

5.1 DEFINITION

In the context of Library and Information resources and services, National Commission on Libraries and Information Science (NCLIS) defines network as" "two or more libraries and /or other organization engaged in a common pattern of information exchange, through communications for some functional purpose" (NCLIS 1975). Today computers are being used to send information across the globe. A standalone computer, which is a very efficient and productive tool by itself, can be made more so by connecting it with other computers. Networking now plays a major role in computing applications.

The process of distributing and processing information among individuals, each with an independent desktop computer being slow and prone to error, led to the concept to connecting computers together to form computer network.

5.2 COMPUTER NETWORKS

A computer network is a communication system where a group of computers and other devices like printers are connected by cables and other hardware. The data is shared between the computers. A network, besides facilitating data communication, allows resources to be shared among all the systems connected to the network.

Computers that are connected in a network can share:

- Data
- Messages
- Printers
- Other hardware resources

Hard Disks
CD-ROM's
Modems

5.2.1 ADVANTAGES OF NETWORKING

(i) Networks allow efficient management of resources.
(ii) Networks help keep information reliable and up-to-date.
(iii) Networks help speed up data sharing.
(iv) Networks allow e-mail service among individuals.

5.2.2 COMPONENTS OF NETWORKS

The common components of all the networks are:

(i) Servers- Computers that provide shared resources provided by a server.
(ii) Clients- Computers that access shared network resources provided by a server.
(iii) Media – The way in which the computers are connected.
(iv) Resources – Files, printers etc. to be used by network users.

Even with these shared components, networks can be divided into two broad categories.

- Server – Based Networks (Dedicated server)
- Peer-to-peer Networks (Non-dedicated server user 10 or less)

In the context of Library and information networks the components may be considered as:

(i) Information resources (collection of a library)
(ii) Clients (type of users)
(iii) Intellectual access system to the documents (i.e. index language)
(iv) Physical access system (delivery of resources to users)
(v) Formal organization

5.3 NEED FOR NETWORKING

- To maximize the utilization of existing information resources
- To provide speedy access to information resources located at different places through communication channels
- For collection control and specialization
- To save funds and avoid duplication

5.4 PERSPECTIVE OF NETWORKS

According to its perspectiveness there are different types of networks

- Protocol perspective
- Application perspective
- Distance perspective
- Physical medium perspective

Library Network Falls Under Application Perspective

Application Networks	(i)	Cooperative Network	Airlines, Railways, Bank Network etc.
	(ii)	Library Network	OCLC, INFLIBNET, DELNET etc.
	(iii)	Public Network	Cable TV Network, TELEX etc.
Library Networks	(i)	International Level	NICNET, INDONET, SIRNET, ERNET etc.
	(ii)	National Level	NICNET, INDONET SIRNET, ERNET etc.
	(iii)	City Level	ADINET, CALIBNET, DELNET etc.
	(iv)	Regional Level	NELIBNET, INFLIBNET, ERNET etc.

5.5 TYPES OF NETWORKS

A network may consist of thousands of computing devices made by various manufactures connected by a variety of transmission media spanning international, and intercontinental boundaries. The networks can be of following types:

- **Private Network**
  Some corporation usually owns these networks that confines access and use of network services to its staff.

- **Cooperative Network**
  This refers to networks that are supported and managed by their users. BITNET is an example of Cooperative networks.
- **ISDN (Integrated Services Digital Network)**
  The development of public data networks for digital communications led to the existence of different networks for different purposes. This resulted in the duplication of networks. To avoid this, interconnection of two or more compatible or incompatible networks to form an Internet is attempted. The main aim of ISDN is to build to a public network providing end-to-end digital connectivity which is capable of supporting a range of digital devices and service, both voice and non voice, on the same basis. This allows users to send and received data text and image from computer systems as well as offering an enhanced telephone service. This is achieved over a single ISDN connection, so that one network can be used for all applications, providing higher speeds of transmission.

But generally depending upon the distance covered in a network, they fall into following types:

5.5.1 LAN
5.5.2 WAN
5.5.3 MAN

5.5.1 LOCAL AREA NETWORK (LAN)

If a network is confined to a single location, typically one building or complex, it is called a Local Area Network (LAN). The maximum distance from one end of a network to another is usually limited by the single strength or the network system's build-in time limit for sending and receiving messages through a physical connection, such as a **Cable.**

LAN is a group of computers in a localized area. A LAN is a network that is typically personal to an organization and is installed for the exclusive use of a particular office or factory of a given organization. It is not often that you will come across two or more organizations in an office complex sharing a LAN.

COMPONENTS OF LAN

When PC is networked, it can access the pooled resources of the network and its capabilities increased manifold. A network encompasses the whole gamut of hardware and software components that make a computer network operative.

Some typical hardware components of LAN are:

(i) Workstations
(ii) Server
(iii) Network Interface Unit
(iv) Communication Channel

(i) **Workstations:** The term workstations refer to the computers that are attached to a LAN and share the resources of the LAN. On a LAN, there can be PCs that do not have either hard disk or floppy disk drives. Such PCs is called "diskless workstations". Such workstations cannot store any data of software. They access them directly from the LAN server. A computer regardless of whether it has disk driver or not is said to become a "node" of the LAN once you attach it to the LAN.

(ii) **Server:** A server is a computer that provides the data, software and hardware resources (like printer) that are shared on the LAN. A LAN can have more than one server. Each server has a unique name on the network and all LAN users identify the server by its name.

- *DEDICATED SERVER:* A server that functions only as a storage area for data and software and allows access to hardware resources is called a dedicated server.
- *NON-DEDICATED SERVER:* In any LANs, the server is just another workstation. Thus, there is a user working on the computer and using it as a workstation and part of the computer also doubles up as a server. Such a server is called a non-dedicated server (since it is not dedicated to serving).

(a) **File Server:** A file server stores files that LAN stations can access. It also decides on the rights and restrictions that the users need to have while accessing files on their own hard disks. The file server regulates the amount of space allowed for each user.

(b) **Printer Server:** A printer server takes care of the printing requirements of a number of workstations. The printer server typically stores the lines to be printed on its disk, and then executes these requests (i.e. prints these files) on a first-in-first-out.

(c) **Modem Server:** A modem server allows LAN users to use a modem to transmit long distance messages.

(iii) **Network Interface Unit (NIU):** NIU is a device that is attached to each of the stations and the server. It helps the workstations and the server. It helps the workstation to establish a connection with the network. Each NIU that is attached to a workstation has a unique number identifying is called the 'Node' address. Thus, the node address of a workstation means the address of the NIU that is attached to the workstation.

(iv) **Communication Channel:** In a LAN, the word communication channel means connecting cables. The connecting cables are the lifelines of LAN. Snap a line is any part of the LAN, and at least a part of the LAN will become in operational.

Some of the communication channels are:

(a) Twisted-pair cables

The oldest and least expensive type of cables used for LANs are the twisted-pair cables. These cables consist of two insulated copper wires twister around each other. E.g. Telephone wires.

(b) Co-axial cables

A co-axial cable consists of one or more cables in a protective covering. These are more expensive than twisted-pair cables but perform better.

(c) Fiber-optic cables

Fiber-optic cables are made of plastic of glass and are as thin as a human hair. These cables are highly durable and offer excellent performance. Their speed of transmission is very high. However, they are expensive and are still not widely used in LAN installations.

Benefits

LANs do not form a network of computers only but also form a network of people. An office, comprising diverse departments and employees in an organization.

(i) *Resource Sharing*

Using a LAN, expensive resources like laser printer, modems, graphic devices and data storage units can be shared.

(ii) *Communication*

Another use of a LAN is that it can help you make the computer do the job of an office intercom. One can use the computer to flash messages on screen of other computers in the office. This would restrict employee's movement from department to department and this saves the time.

(iii) *Security*

The PC is capable of storing a fair amount of information, but it is not a very secure place to store data. Using a LAN, users can store their files on a computer that is part of the LAN. A LAN has build-in security features such that it would be virtually impossible for anyone to get hold of these files.

(iv) *Expanded PC Usage*

A LAN is very accommodating. It takes into consideration the fact that employees can get transferred between departments, or machine can be moved to different locations. New machines can be added, or existing once removed. A LAN ensures that, despite these changes, a user goes through minimum inconvenience and continues to benefit from the LAN.

5.5.2 WIDE AREA NETWORK (WAN)

As the advantage of networking became known, business saw the need to expand the networks. LANs could not adequately support the network needs of a large business, with offices and operations spread over a wide area. This led to the development of Wide Area Networks (WAN).

When a network is spread over wide areas, such as across cities, states of countries, it is called a Wide Area Network (WAN). Communication on WAN takes place via telephone lines, satellites or micro-wave links rather than through a physical cable.

Comparison

Sl. No.	*LAN*	*WAN*
1	Confined to a single location	Spread over to wide areas
2	Message sending and receiving through cable	Messages sending and receiving through telephone lines, satellites, microwave links
3	Small community of users are served	Large community users are served

5.5.3 METROPOLITAN AREA NETWORK (MAN)

In between LAN and WAN is the Metropolitan Area Network (MAN). A MAN is a network that covers an entire city, but uses LAN technology. Cable television networks are examples of MAN's distributing television signals. The MAN's are interested in carrying information in the form of computer signals from one computer to another.

5.6 NETWORK TOPOLOGY

There are several different ways to organize the computers to form a network. These organizations of the computers in a network are referred to as network topology. These include:

5.6.1 Star Topology
5.6.2 Ring Topology
5.6.3 Bus Topology
5.6.4 Mesh Topology
5.6.5 Hierarchical Topology

5.6.1 **Star Topology:** In a star topology, server computer is situated at the center and all workstations are connected directly to it. Here, all the messages are sent through the server. When we send a message from one computer to another, it must go through the server. If the server fails, all networks are held up.

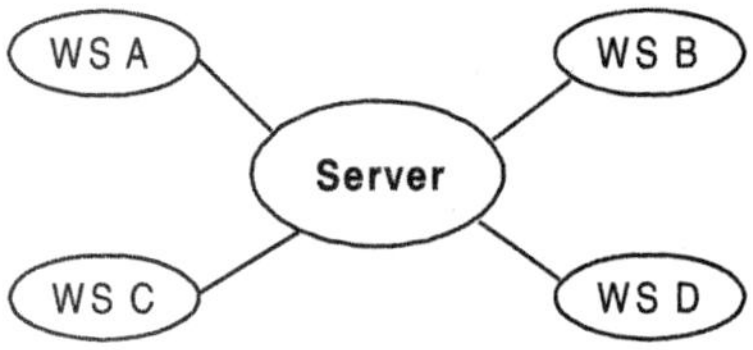

5.6.2 **Ring Topology:** In ring network topology, the computers and peripheral devices are arranged in a ring like fashion. Here, any computer can communicate with any other computer by sending a signal around the ring. As the message is sent, each computer determines whether it is its message, if not, it is shifted to other computer. It is very similar to Bus topology but the only difference is that here a complete loop of the cable is formed.

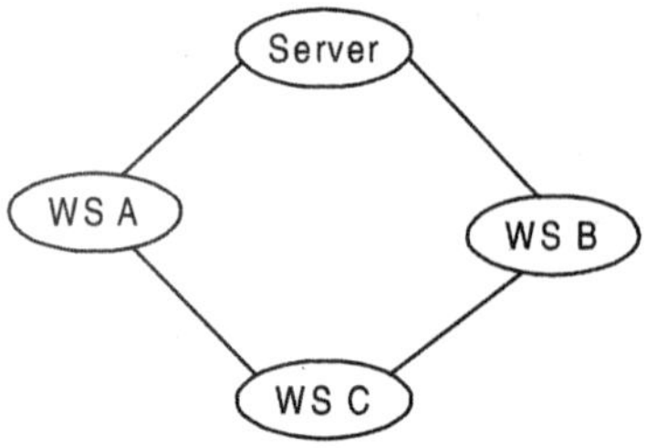

5.6.3 **Bus Topology:** In this type of topology the computers are connected by a cable known is as bus and messages are sent along this bus cable. In this topology, the failure of a single computer does not affect the performance of rest of the network.

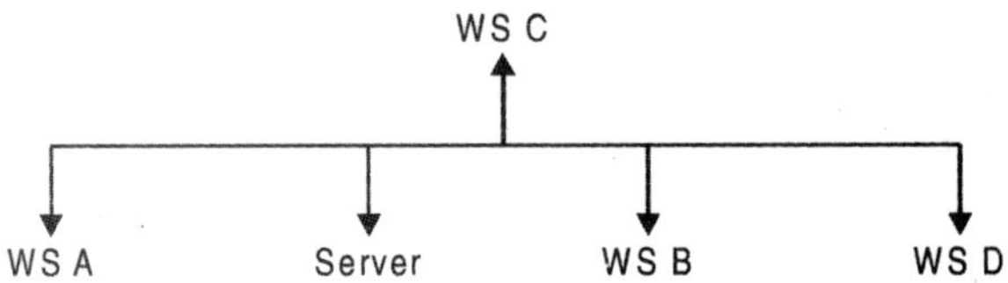

5.6.4 **Mesh Topology:** This topology has multiplicity of paths from server to workstations and permits any two devices to communicate directly within network. It is very dependable because it provides multiple roots into and out of each location. Although this is an expensive one but some users prefer the reliability of this network in comparison of other ones, especially for networks with only a few nodes or workstations.

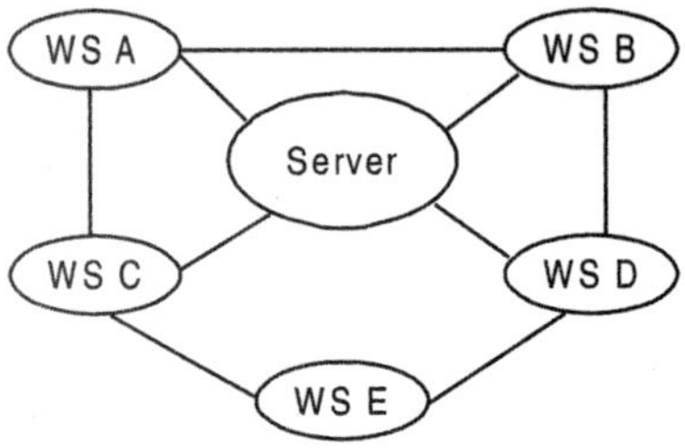

5.6.5 **Hierarchical Topology:** It is also called as tree topology where server computer is situated at the highest order of the hierarchy and workstations are connected in a tree like hierarchical fashion. But the drawback of this topology is that if upper level computer fails to work, the complete network working is held up.

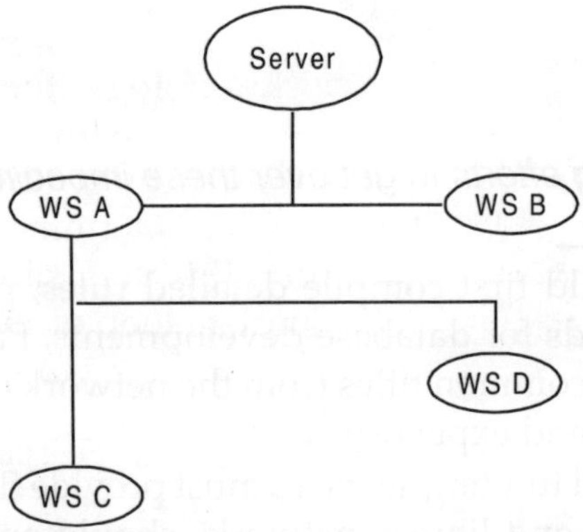

Data transfer using mesh topology is faster than all topologies. Mesh networks are also quite fault resistant. If a particular path fails, data can be routed via alternate paths.

5.7 ADVANTAGES

The host computer can be interacted by large number of spread over terminals. It can give access to databases, retrieve the information and even get the information in printed form. The retrieval information can be recorded in floppies. It'll give on-line and e-mail facility. It helps to facilitate the resource sharing within no time.

5.8 IMPEDIMENTS

The main problems faced by the Indian libraries are:

- It is difficult to enforce standards in data conversion.
- Even after using the uniform input format and data entry procedure, there could be a significant variation in indexing; and assigning keywords.
- Large libraries would be unwilling to become part of the system.
- Non-availability of staff with adequate expertise and enough training facilities in the country.
- Libraries that have already created databases using their own input formats and other rules and procedures would be reluctant to change them due to the cost of inputs required for effecting the change.
- Inadequate resources for acquiring the hardware, software and other facilities for joining the network.

- Many libraries do not have the software, which is tailored to their procedures and which can function efficiently and effectively in a WAN environment. They look for integrated software for library automation and database development.
- Many libraries do not get adequate support from the management.

5.9 SOLUTIONS

Library networks are making efforts to get over these impediments:

(i) The Networks should first compile detailed rules, procedures keeping in view the existing standards for database developments. Participating libraries should download the most common titles from the network office/databases, which will save human efforts and expenditure.

(ii) The Government and funding agencies must provide financial support for database creation in libraries and library networks should approach the GOI to provide allocation of budget in the annual and five year plans.

(iii) The Networks should lay down some guidelines to share their resources among large and small libraries by lending and borrowing arrangements.

(iv) The Networks management should organize practical based programs for the staff of the participating libraries.

(v) The Networks management should also provide common software on a cost-to-cost basis as well as technical support to participating libraries.

(vi) The Networks should encourage database development contractors to come up in large numbers to create databases on contract including retrospective conversion. This would speed up the time consuming task of data conversion.

REFERENCES

1. Aswal, RS, ed. – Information Networks in India, New Delhi: Ess Ess Publication, 2003.
2. Barness, J, Susan – Becoming a Digital Library, New York: Marcel Decker, 2002.
3. Baruah, A – Computer Networking in Libraries, Delhi: Kalpaz, 2002.
4. Desikan, RS and Muthuswamy, R – Configuring a Local Area Network System for a Technical Information Center: A Case Study, *IN* AGLIS Journal, Vol. 8, No. 1-4, 1991.
5. Elashami, AM – Networking CD-ROMs: The Decision Makers Guide to Local Area Network Solutions, New York: American Library Association, 1996.
6. Jebaraj, Franklin David and Devadoss, Fredrick Robin – Library and Information Networks in India, in Library Philosophy and Practice, Vol. 6, No. 2 (Spring 2004).

7. Murthy, SS et al. ed. – Bibliographic Databases and Networks : Proceedings of the International Conference 1989/Organized by DESIDOC, New Delhi : Tata McGraw Hill, 1990.

8. Vashishth, CP ed. – Computerisation and Library Network, New Delhi: ILA, 1991.

9. Tripathi, SM – Documentation and Information Services and Networks, Vol. 2, Information Systems and Networks, Agra: Y.K. Publishers, 1997.

10. Web sites: inflibnet.ac.in; btisnet.nic.in; mylibnet.org; calibnet.org; alibnet.org; elnet.nic.in; indonet.net; lucklibnet.com ; ugc.ac.in; home.nic.in; ernet.in; unesco.org

CHAPTER 6

LIBRARY AND INFORMATION NETWORKS

The explosion in the amount of literature that is available, increases among the number of users and their different needs, and the application of electronic media are forcing libraries to construct and participate in networks. Magnetic tapes, floppy disks, and CD-ROMs provide enough data storage capacity. Retrieval through telecommunication networks and access to international databases are available for searching for information on various subjects. With the advent of networks, remote transmission of texts and graphics, video clips and animated clips are also possible.

6.1 DEFINITION

- A library network is broadly described as a group of libraries coming together with some agreement of understanding to help each other with a view to satisfying the information needs of their clientele.
- UNISIST II working document defines Information Network as a set of inter-related information systems associated with communication facilities, which are cooperating through more or less formal agreements in order to implement information handling operations to offer better services to the users.
- The National Commission on Libraries & Information Science in its National Programme Document (1975) defines a network as two or more libraries engaged in a common pattern of information exchange, through communications for some functional purpose.

6.2 OBJECTIVES

- To promote and support adoption of standards in library operations.
- To create databases for projects, specialists and institutions to provide online information services.
- To improve the efficiency of housekeeping operations.
- To coordinate with other regional, national & international network for exchange of information and documents.
- To generate new services and to improve the efficiency of existing ones.

6.3 NETWORK DEVELOPMENT

Some factors that are responsible for the development of library and information networks in India are:

- The report of the working group of the Planning Commission on modernization of library services and informatics for the seventh five year plan, 1985-90.
- The National Policy on Library & Information systems document (1986) accepted by the ministry of HRD, Government of India.
- The report on national policy on university libraries prepared by the Association of Indian Universities (1987).
- The UGC report on information systems for science and technology under the Department of Science & Industrial Research (DSIR) Government of India has been vigorously promoting an integrated approach to library automation and networking.

Growth of Indian Library Networks

1951 The need for developing libraries in a proper manner had always been emphasized from the First five year plan of the country initiated in 1951.

1958 "Scientific Policy Resolution" adopted at the instance of Pt. Jawaharlal Nehru emphasized the forecasting of scientific temper in people. In pursuance of this agenda, several committees and commissions were appointed to look into scientific issues and come up with necessary recommendations.

1959 Sinha Committee Report.

1965 S.R. Ranganathan Report to UGC.

1971 Peter Lazar Report and V.A. Kamat Report.

1973 National Informatics Centre began its work with the objectives to design, develop and implement advanced computer-based methodologies; to promote adoption of computer based data management technologies; to generate specialized manpower in the field of Informatics; and to build intracity and intercity computer network in the country for interconnecting various Ministries/Departments of Central Government with those of states and associated semi-government and autonomous organizations for setting up of a distributed governmental information system.

1977 NISSAT began to play its role as a decentralized system to promote standardized and mutually compatible information system for collection, storages, processing and dissemination of information.

1983 Technology Policy Statement emphasized the need for a technology information base.

1984 Working Group of the Planning Commission headed by Dr. N. Seshagiri recommended to the Govt., the need for modernization of library services and Informatics during the 7th Five year plan 1985-1990.

1988 National Policy on Library and Information Systems recommended, among other things using information technology in a national level.

1997-2002 Working Group of Planning Commission on Library and informatics for the 9th Five year plans 1997-2002 which was prepared under the chairmanship of Mr. B.P. Singh, Secretary, Department of Culture, is an important report, as we have to modernize the libraries to take up challenges of 21st century scenario of information technology, Networking and INTERNET.

6.4 LIMITATIONS

A network may fail in the early stages if there is no proper planning or if adequate funds are not available. Moreover, a common memorandum of agreement signed by the participating libraries at the institutional level is essential for the success of a network venture. On a more practical level, catalog data must be in a standard, machine readable form for it to be shared and exchanged. And, finally, a continuous flow of external assistance is crucial for the network's survival.

6.5 INDIAN NETWORKS*

6.5.1 General Networks in India
6.5.2 Metropolitan Networks
6.5.3 Wide Area Network

6.5.1 GENERAL NETWORKS IN INDIA

- **NICNET: National Information Center Network/Sponsor: Planning Commission, Govt. of India.**
  Membership: Four national and regional nodes, 32 state and union territory nodes; seventy cities and towns
  Services: Bulk file transfer; teleconferencing; full text and bibliographic retrieval services
  Application: ICMRNIC Center; MEDLARS in India; Chemical Abstracts database
- **INDONET: INDONET data Network/Sponsor: CMC Ltd. (1986) = Informatics India Ltd. (1989)**
  Membership: Commercial computer network
  Services: Database services such as DIALOG, COMPUSERVE; IP; SHARP
  Applications: ACME; file transfer; international gateway
- **I – NET (VIKRAM): I – NET/Sponsor: Dept. of Telecommunications, Govt. of India**
  Connectivity: Packet switched public data network covering nine cities
  Services: Information exchange through e-mail/FTP; Bibliographic databases

6.5.2 METROPOLITAN NETWORKS

- **CALIBNET: Calcutta Libraries Network/Sponsor: NISSAT – Govt. of India**
  Applications: Cataloging; serials control; acquisitions; circulation
  Services: CAS; SDI; union catalog; partial database; editing and retrieval of records; global information; search; full-text document delivery; library automation; CALIBNET INFO Services
- **BONET: Bombay Library Network/Sponsor: NISSAT & NCST (1994)**
  Objective: To promote cooperation among libraries in Bombay
  Services: online catalog; online document delivery; IRS; interlibrary loan; dissemination of information
- **DELNET : Developing Library Network/Sponsor: NISSAT & NIC (1988)**
  Objective: To promote resource sharing; develop a network of libraries; collect, store, disseminate information
  Members: 165 Institutions, 600 Libraries, 15 States in India, 5 from outside India
  Services: resource sharing; free Software; ICE online facility; books database; thesis database; Indian specialists; database
- **ADINET : Ahmedabad Library Network/Sponsor: NISSAT, DSIR (1994) & INFLIBNET**
  Objective: To bring cooperation among its regional libraries; to develop

databases; to integrate scientific and technical information systems
Members: 9 libraries
Services: library automation; library holdings; database in progress

- **MYLIBNET : Mysore Library Network/Sponsor: NISSAT (1994)**
  Objective: Developing software tools; conducting seminar; workshops/ training programs; conduct surveys
  Host Site: CFTRI, Mysore
  Members: 116 Institutions
  Services: MYLIB Database; E-journals; food patents; CFTRI Library Bulletin; public services.

6.5.3 WIDE AREA NETWORK

- **DESINET: Defense Science Information Network/Sponsor: DESIDOC, Delhi**
  Activity: Focus on scientific, research and defense communities
- **ERNET: Educational and Research Network/Dept. of Electronics, Govt. of India; UNESCO (Financial assistance from UNDP)**
  Members: 8 institutions (5 IITs, IISc., National Centre for Software Technology – Bombay, CCI wing of Dept. of Electronics)
  Services: Communication services such as e-mail, file transfer, remote log on, database access, bulletin board etc.
- **SIRNET: Scientific and Industrial Research Network/CSIR (Commissioned Agency- NCST, Bombay)**
  Members: 40 labs and R&D Institutions
  Applications: scientific communication; leather technology; natural products; food technology; medicinal plants
- **VIDYANET: VIDYANET (Dedicated Communication Computer Net)/Sponsor: TATA Institute of Fundamental Research, Bombay**
  Objectives: To provide rapid means of communications by linking computers at various institutions in India to similar networks outside the country; to stimulate corporate research, the day-to-day exchange of research information and the execution of joint projects and publications
  Services: File transfer facility; sharing of computer resources and access to remote applications, databases, libraries, etc.
- **BTISNET (Specialized Information Network) /Sponsor: Dept. of Biotechnology, Govt. of India**
  Connectivity: 10 Specialized Information Centres in genetic engineering, plant tissue culture; photosynthesis and plant molecular biology; cell transformation; bio-process engineering.

Services: Data processing using applications software; online communication access; facsimile facility

- **INFLIBNET: Information Library Network/Sponsor: UGC (1991)**

  Connectivity: computer communication network of universities and R&D; libraries and bibliographic information centers throughout the country

  Members: 200 Universities; 400 College libraries; 200 R&D libraries

  Services: catalog service; database Services; document supply services; e-mail; BBS: audio and video conferencing, etc.

- **BALNET: Bangalore Library Network/ Sponsor: JRD Tata Memorial Library (1995)**

  Members: 100 Libraries

  Services: CD-ROM database searching, On-line Union Catalogue of Periodicals Request System for ILL, Searching of Foreign database, E-mail and Internet Access, Software for OPAC

- **MALIBNET: Madras Library Network /Sponsor: INSDOC & NISSAT (1993)**

  Members: 15 Libraries

  Activity: Two important databases, a directory database of current serials in Madras and a contents database covering articles published in 300 journals available in Madras libraries.

6.6 CALIBNET (CALCUTTA LIBRARY NETWORK)

CALIBNET, a Government of India project, has been launched by the National Information Systems for Science and Technology NISSAT, Department of Scientific & Industrial Research (DSIR); and managed by the CALIBNET Society established under the West Bengal Government's Societies Registration Act, 1961.

CALIBNET aims to provide the individual libraries and their reading members with cost-effective solutions to their information problems.

The primary objective of the project is building access to library & information resources available in the eastern region. This has been pursued through : Implementation of a series of Databases, Bibliographic, Factual and Intellectual Assets of West Bengal.

This apart, CALIBNET provides its Participating Members and the user community at large with the following:

- Active links in this Web-Page to access
- Indian Library & Network Resources
- Overseas Library Resources on India

- Worldwide Library Catalogues
- National Libraries of the World
- Newspapers & Journals
- Electronic Reference Tools
- Factual Information Sources
- Document Supply Services, & Varied Programs for:
  - (i) On Demand Information Services
  - (ii) Consultative Service for Library Automation
  - (iii) Manpower Development Opportunities, and
  - (iv) Research & Development in IT Applications

Structure

Basically CALIBNET is a network with distributed approach to services. Each participant Library would collect, process and hold information on local computers which are connected with the another through X 23 packet switched network. One of the network participants network service centre will be responsible for global i.e. within the network user service and also act to network control centre. Standardization may be based on UNIX operating system. For this purpose INSDOC Regional Centre is identified to act as Network Service Centre (NSC).

Functions

CALIBNET has planned to organize a number of activities such as electronic mail, file transfer, remote log on and database and documents access. In addition, within the individual libraries, the functions to be automated are cataloguing, serials control, acquisition and fund accounting, circulation and local user services. The networking provides for global user services (covering all the members of the user libraries) of current awareness, SDI, union catalogues, partial databases and accesses to national and international network.

6.7 DELNET

(Developing Library Network - formally named as Delhi Library Network)

DELNET has been in operation since January 1988 and was registered as a society in 1992. It was initially sponsored by the National Information System for Science and Technology (NISSAT), Department of Scientific and Industrial Research, Government of India and is currently being promoted by the National Informatics Centre, Department of Information Technology, Ministry of Communications and Information Technology, Government of India and India International Centre, New Delhi.

DELNET has been established with the prime objective of promoting resource sharing among the libraries through the development of a network of libraries. It aims to collect, store, and disseminate information besides offering computerised services to users, to coordinate efforts for suitable collection development and also to reduce unnecessary duplication wherever possible.

DELNET has been actively engaged with the compilation of various Union Catalogues of the resources available in member-libraries. It has already created the Union Catalogue of Books, Union List of Current Periodicals, Union Catalogue of Periodicals, CD-ROM Database, Database of Indian Specialists, Database of Periodical Articles, Union List of Video Recordings, Urdu Manuscripts' Database, Database of Theses and Dissertations, DEVINSA Database, sample databases of language publications using GIST technology and several other databases. The data is being updated in each of these databases and is growing rapidly. All the DELNET databases have been resident on DELSIS, an in-house software developed on BASIS Plus, an RDBMS, the product of Information Dimensions Inc. of USA which has been provided to DELNET courtesy National Informatics Centre, New Delhi.

DELNET provides an array of facilities including e-mail to its member libraries including both institutional and associate institutional members. DELNET'S relentless efforts in resource sharing have proved extremely effective. It has indeed been a big leap towards the modernisation of libraries in India.

The Main Objectives of DELNET are:

- To promote sharing of resources among the libraries by developing a network of libraries, by collecting, storing and disseminating information and by offering computerised services to the users;
- To undertake scientific research in the area of Information Science and Technology, create new systems in the field, apply the results of research and publish them;
- To offer technical guidance to the member-libraries on collecting, storing, sharing and disseminating information;
- To coordinate efforts for suitable collection development and reduce unnecessary duplication wherever possible;
- To establish/facilitate the establishment of referral and /or research centres, and maintain a central online union catalogue of books, serials and non-book materials of all the participating libraries;
- To facilitate and promote delivery of documents manually or mechanically;
- To develop specialised bibliographic database of books, serials and non-book materials;
- To develop databases of projects, specialists and institutions;
- To possess and maintain electronic and mechanical equipment for speedy communication of information and delivery of electronic mail;

- To coordinate with other regional, national and international networks and libraries for exchange of information and documents;

The Services: Online Databases (Online)

- Union Catalogue of Books : CCF
- Union Catalogue of Books : MARC Format
- Union List of Current Periodicals
- Union Catalogue of Periodicals
- Database of Periodical Articles
- Indian Specialists : A Who's who
- CD-ROM Database
- Union List of Video Recordings
- Union List of Sound Recordings
- Union List of Newspapers
- Union List of Serials: Management Libraries
- Union List of Serials : Petroleum and Natural Gas
- Union List of Hindi Books
- Multilingual Books: Sample Database
- Urdu Manuscripts Database
- Database of Theses and Dissertations
- DEVINSA Database

The Other Services

- ILL Online
- Retro conversion
- Referral Services
- Creation and Maintenance of bibliographic databases
- Document Delivery Services
- Document Delivery Services
- Training programmes
- Lectures and Workshops
- Newsletter
- DELSIS (DELNET for Information Services)
- DELSEARCH: An Offline e-mail Based Remote Database Access System
- DEL DOS
- DEL PLUS
- DEL MARC

Internet

- Electronic Mail
- Full INTERNET (TCP/IP)

Products: Online Databases

Union Catalogue of Books on CCF

DELNET maintains an online union catalogue of books available in its member-libraries. This union catalogue is continuously updated and is growing in size. The information can be retrieved by author, title, subject, conference, series, etc. It has **28,55,821** bibliographic records. The request for inter-library loan can be placed through the online system.

Union Catalogue of Books: MARC Format

MARC is an internationally used format for machine readable bibliographic records. DELNET has introduced CCF for the creation of records in MARC format. It has presently **44,132** records. DELNET has separately created a union catalogue of books for MARC records.

Union List of Current Periodicals

DELNET has created union lists of current periodicals in science and technology, social sciences and humanities. This database is available online to DELNET users. It now lists **21,402** periodicals and is regularly updated and new titles are added annually.

Union Catalogue of Periodicals

DELNET maintains a union catalogue of periodicals, which contains full holdings data of the libraries. At present, the database contains **19,289** records.

Database of Periodical Articles

The database has details of articles which can be searched under the title, author, compiler, name of the periodical and subject. The database is being extensively utilised by the researchers and scholars. At present the database contains **5, 69,583** records.

Indian Specialist's Database

DELNET has created a database of Indian specialists which is available online to the members. This database now has 2,000 records of eminent scientists, educationists and writers from all over the country and is growing. The bibliographical details like name, address, phone, fax, e-mail address, qualifications, subject specialisation, languages known, areas of interest, awards received, etc. on each specialist are available in this database. The questionnaires are being sent periodically to the specialists excelling in diverse fields of knowledge.

CD-ROM Database

A bibliographic database of CD-ROMs available with the member-libraries has been started recently and is available online. There are **2,106** records.

Union List of Video Recordings

This is a database of video cassettes available in DELNET member libraries and has about **3,667** listings.

Union List of Sound Recordings

This union list consists of **748** audio- cassette records available in member-libraries.

Union List of Newspapers

This database lists newspapers being subscribed by Delhi Libraries. It contains information about the newspapers including title, name of the editor, published from, e-mail address and also the web address of the INTERNET edition, if available. There are 70 records in this database.

Union List of Serials of Management Libraries

DELNET has recently constituted a Sub-committee for rationalising the periodicals in the Management Sector Libraries in and around Delhi. It contains nearly 800 serials.

Union Catalogue of Hindi Books

The database contains nearly 3,000 records in Hindi and can be retrieved through the GIST compatible system.

Multilingual Books : Sample Database

DELNET has prepared a sample database of language publications of various Indian and some foreign languages using GIST technology. This acts as a guideline for member-libraries wanting to create databases other than in English.

Urdu Manuscripts' Database

DELNET has created an Urdu manuscripts' database which is available online to member-libraries and lists **210** manuscripts. It contains a descriptive bibliography on a variety of subjects such as animal husbandry, astronomy, teaching techniques, ethics, Arabian history, letter writing, literary criticism, Islamic sects, Jehad, theology, sports, etc. the maximum number of entries are on poetry, fiction and Islam.

Database of Theses and Dissertations

DELNET has recently started the database on theses and dissertations available in various member-libraries. This database is steadily growing in size and now has **41,420** records.

DEVINSA Database

DELNET is provides the access to DEVINSA database which contains nearly 20,000 records for journal articles, books (including analyticals) and unpublished materials on socio-economic issues in South Asian countries.

Serials: Petroleum and Natural Gas

A serials database on the current periodicals available in Petroleum and Natural Gas Libraries in India has been started recently and is available online. It has nearly 1,000 records.

The Other Services

ILL Online

DELNET members can place their inter-library loan requests through our ILL Online facility, which is available on the union catalogue of books database. The members' requests appear on the main server, which are monitored by DELNET staff at regular intervals and the books are acquired and supplied to the requesting library through the courier. The charges for this service are Rs.4000/- per year. Photocopying charges for journal articles and courier charges for sending books to member-libraries outside Delhi are extra.

Retro-Conversion

DELNET offers retro conversion facilities to the libraries for the creation of MARC records.

Referral Services

DELNET maintains a referral centre that provides reference facilities to participating libraries. The referral centre also looks after the access to the central databases and monitors access to international databases.

Creation and Maintenance of Bibliographic Databases

DELNET helps the participating libraries in the creation of bibliographic databases. It is considered that for effective networking, standard bibliographic data should be available in machine readable form to the libraries. Periodic meetings of the member-librarians are organised to discuss their problems.

Document Delivery Services

DELNET provides the Document Delivery Services to its users and it is a very popular.

Training Programmes

DELNET has organised in collaboration with NIC Monthly Training Programmes since September 2001 on the topics covering MARC21, Web Page Designing & Hosting, Internet Searching Strategies, Library Resources on the Internet and CDROM Networking. A large number of library and information science professionals from different parts of India had attended these programmes.

DELNET also conducts training programmes in the use of DELNET services, software, e-mail, AACR2 and LC Subject Headings, Internet, etc. from time to time. Information about future training programmes is available on request.

Lectures and Workshops

DELNET organises lectures by networking specialists working in different parts of the world. The lectures are open to members, specialists and users in general. DELNET also organises national workshops, seminars and meets on library networking periodically.

Newsletter

DELNET publishes a Newsletter in order to spread the message and increase the awareness about library networking in India. Through this Newsletter, DELNET communicates to its members the progress it is making in various fields. The Newsletter is also a forum for communication on the advances, achievements and needs of the libraries and their services.

Internet

Electronic Mail

DELNET provides **RENNIC e-mail facility** to its member-libraries which is introduced by National Informatics Centre. This gives them access to both national and international e-mail users and also to INTERNET users. The e-mail service is very efficient, fast and effective.

INTERNET (TCP/IP) Connectivity

DELNET provides INTERNET TCP/IP Connectivity which is given to member-libraries in Delhi through NIC at Rs. 5,600 per year for 500 hours of connect time. These rates are subject to change by NIC.

Softwares

Delsis

A major breakthrough has been achieved by DELNET with the launch of DELSIS, a powerful library networking software. DELSIS (DELNET system for Information Services) is an integrated modular system which supports DELNET online databases.

DELSIS has been developed by DELNET on a Relational Database Management System called BASISplus provided by NIC.DELSIS handles not only the Online Public Access Catalogue but also has the administrative tools for building up the union catalogues on BASISplus. It provides powerful and extensive facilities for online enquiries for books, serials, biographical details about the specialists and supports the cataloguing of books in Indian languages.

Salient Features of DELSIS:

- DELSIS is a user-friendly, menu-driven package.
- Its versatile options allow the users to retrieve the information quickly.
- It contains the modules for Online Public Access Catalogue as well as the modules for the creation of databases, e.g. addition, deletion, importing of records, etc.
- The Online Public Access Catalogue (OPAC) components of DELSIS can meet the needs of the users, irrespective of whether the user has negligible computer experience or is familiar with using computers to perform various library tasks.

DEL-DOS

DEL-DOS based on DOS platform is used for creating MARC records of books published in English as well as for creating records in Indian languages using GIST card. Some of its salient features are:

- The software is very simple and easy to use.
- The records can be stored in MARC format.
- Deletion and printing of selective and range of records is possible.
- Global values can be defined during the worksheet entry.
- The search results can be displayed in the Tag Format, AACR-II or the brief summary can also be displayed and stored or printed out.
- The name authority database is maintained.
- Import/Export into and from ISO 2709 is possible.

DEL-PLUS

DELNET is pleased to announce the release of DEL-PLUS Version 1.0.0 after the successful creation and implementation of DELSIS Unix version. It is an efficient tool for creating and retrieving bibliographic databases and catalogues.

DEL-PLUS can convert the simple PC into a powerful management information system. Some of the salient features are:

- It is simple and easy to use. The novice library professionals and end users can interact with the software without any prior training.
- It is user-friendly with adequate window-menus for data inputting and search capabilities.
- It provides the option for creating the bibliographic records either using Common Communication Format (CCF) or the MARC Format.

DEL-PLUS provides the following operational modules:

(a) **Database Creation and Maintenance**
This is used to create and store the bibliographic records in a machine readable format using CCF or MARC format so as to facilitate the easier exchange of information.

Salient Features

(1) The desirable formats worksheet, i.e. CCF or MARC worksheets can be chosen for data storage purpose.
(2) The MARC worksheet consists of two levels, viz. fixed field entry and variable field entry. To save the user's time and also the system space, the required field tags along with the indicators can be chosen.
(3) The online assistance is available for data inputting through the help menus.
(4) Data validation check is possible in order to avoid the data errors.
(5) Provision for duplicate checking is available while inputting or importing a record into a database.

(6) The authority database is maintained.
(7) Data Import/Export into and from MARC as well as CCF is made possible.
(8) The option for printing the desired records is also available.

(b) **Online Public Access Catalogue (OPAC)**

This module helps the librarians as well as the end users to retrieve the information available in the database in a very user-friendly manner.

Salient Features

(1) Browsing facility: Available for beginners. They can search a book by title, author, subject, etc.
(2) Word or phrase searching.
(3) Full text searching.
(4) Search Term is not case sensitive.
(5) Brief as well as detailed bibliographical information can be retrieved.
(6) Displays records in AACR II format.
(7) Print search results in standard AACR II format or other formats as desired.

We are sure that DEL-PLUS will become a very popular software for libraries interested in creating standard bibliographic records.

Del-marc

Del-marc Ver 1.0.0

This is basically for the bigger libraries which are complex entities with a large collection and serving a huge clientele. To carry out various operations in a library effectively, there is a need for automation. This software has been designed after a comprehensive study of different library- related functions performed in different kinds of libraries. This software is quite easy to work with. The software comprises the following modules:

Benefits of Using Del-marc 1.0.0

1. Available at a greatly reduced cost.
2. Software designed and developed exclusively to work under all kinds of libraries such as public, academic and special libraries.
3. Multi user facility of this software will allow different branch libraries/sections/nodes to function together.
4. Free updation/modification.
5. Free technical assistance.
6. Follows internationally recommended standards and formats such as US-MARC, UNI-MARC, UK-MARC, MARC 2, CCF, AACR- II

Software Modules

- Acquisition
- Cataloguing
- Circulation
- OPAC
- Administration
- Export/Import
- Authority Control
- Article Indexing
- Reports

Acquisition: The acquisition module enables library staff to handle the following major functions related to acquisition of library material :

- Suggestions management
- Approval
- Ordering, cancellation and reminders
- Receiving
- Accessioning
- Management of vendors, publishers and currency tables.

Cataloguing: The cataloguing module enables you to catalogue any type of material in any of the MARC formats.

Circulation: This module will take care of all possible functions like issue, return, reissue, reservation, etc. Member enquiry, maintenance of status of material can be handled. Complex functions like fare management for each category of user and material can also be effectively carried out.

OPAC: It Facilitates Three Types of Functions

1. Individual search (Search by Author, Title, ISBN, Acc. No., Subject, Class No. etc)
2. Boolean search (Search by Author, Title, ISBN, Acc. No., Subject, Class No. etc in combination)
3. Special search (For cataloguing purposes).
4. Results can be seen in AACR-II format or any MARC format described above.

Administration: Here you can define the categories, group, and their exchange, sales, acquisition modes, MARC tags, holidays, user passwords etc. that will be used throughout the functioning of the software.

Export/Import: Here you can export/import your data into/from any standard MARC format described above.

Authority Control: This module enables you to maintain author, title, series and subject authorities.

Article Indexing: This module is developed to maintain various articles in the library or out of the library.

Reports: Here you will get each and every type of report such as vendors' list, material ordered, material received, order due, overdue charges, stock verification, etc. Reports can also be generated date wise.

6.8 INFLIBNET

University Grants Commission started INFLIBNET Programme as a project of Inter-University Centre for Astronomy and Astrophysics (IUCAA), Poona in April, 1991 with its headquarter at Ahmedabad to promote resource development, sharing and its efficient utilisation at national level satisfying the complex and ever increasing needs of the user. The programme is a major national effort to improve information access and transfer capabilities and aim to establish a cooperative computer communication network for linking libraries and information centres in academic, research and development institutions and other organisation of national importance. It organises service providing precise search, speedy access and faster dissemination of information and extend the access to the information resources with equity and efficiency for the users in the system characterised by diversity, accessibility and quality.

Programme was started giving highest priority to manpower development. Accordingly, during the last three years INFLIBNET has organised 14 training courses for library staff from various academic institutions and their managers. The generation of standards, particularly standards for data capturing was another important activity which needed immediate attention. It has helped initiating development of national database of library resources. We are at present concentrating on computerisation of libraries and creation of computerised databases to take advantage of networking facilities. The Programme is being implemented in phases and 69 universities have already been provided grant for computerisation and networking of libraries. The universities, which could not be covered so far, have been provided grant for procurement of core on-line information access facilities to enable them to share information with others. A central database (union catalogue) comprising 28000 serial, 50,000 theses and about 2.5 lakhs book holdings has been created from the data received from about 69 universities. We have also created a database of experts in various academic disciplines in the country. A number of library application software and utilities packages have been developed for library management and creation of union catalogue. Development of Integrated Library Management Software (ILMS) is in progress and is being completed shortly. It is proposed to extend INFLIBNET services through available Data communication networks in the country. This will provide a basic platform to academic libraries for on-line sharing of information. INFLIBNET is already providing various off-line and on-line services, which includes an off- line service known as Contents with Abstracts of Scientific and Technical journal (COPSAT) in collaboration with National Centre for Science Information (NCSI).

The Ministry gave approval for converting the project of INFLIBNET Programme into an Inter-University Centre under Article 12(CCC) of UGC Act in August, 1995. INFLIBNET Centre has now been registered as an autonomous society and has become a regular Inter- University Çentre of University Grants Commission since May 1996.

- About Objectives
- Role of INFLIBNET.
- Role of RC.
- DRC
- SIC
- Participation in INFLIBNET.
- Funding
- Governance

Objectives of INFLIBNET

- Moderenise libraries/information centres in the country.
- Establish a mechanism for information transfer and access.
- Support scholarship and academic work.
- Facilitate pooling, sharing & optimisation of Library/information resources.
- Organise library services at macro level, affordable cost and maximise benifits.
- Provide speedy and efficient services to end users.
- The ultimate aim is to provide the end users a mechanism for sharing and using information resources exploiting modern information technology.

Role of INFLIBNET

- To generate awareness about the applications of computer for the library and information activities and promote modernisation of libraries.
- To provide technical assistance in system definition establishment of computerised facilities and networking of libraries.
- To up-skill library staff and their managers in computerised library operation and management of computerised libraries through regular training programmes.
- To establish computer/communication networking of libraries and information centres using existing facilities such as I-NET, ERNET and NICNET etc.
- To computerise and network libraries and information centres in all universities.
- Creation of academic databases as a national resource and its updation.

Establish Resource Centres:

1. Sectorial Information Centres (SIC) for detailed subject specific information.
2. Document Resource Centres (DRC) for Document Delivery service.
3. Establish regional centres and other infrastructure to organise services.

Role of Regional Centre

- Provide help to members in the region in the computerisation of libraries and networking.
- Create bibliographical databases of library materials by pooling computerised data from INFLIBNET members.
- Create special databases e.g. Database of Experts, Institutions, Projects, etc. in the region.
- Pool Data from all other regions and provide services to the members in their region.
- Coordinate cooperative acquisition of costly books and periodicals in the respective region.
- Organise on-site training and assist libraries in improving and enhancing their services.

Role of Document Resource Centre

- Existing resources as and where available to be used to organise document delivery services.
- Rich and resourceful universities to be identified to act as Document Resource Centre (DRC).
- DRCs will be equipped with facility for on-line and off-line delivery of documents e.g. xeroxing facility, networking facility etc. to provide services to all the members at nominal cost.

Role of Sectoral Information Centre

- To provide subject specific information to the users. Three information centres already set up by University Grants Commission to be utilised for services.
- National Centre for Science Information, Bangalore for Science and Technology.
- MS University, Baroda for social sciences.
- SNDT Women's University, Bombay for Humanities.
- Procure and provide CD-ROM/Data based information services.
- Establish and coordinate Bulletin Board and subject specific electronic forum services.

Other information centres e.g. NISSAT/CSIR, INSDOC, DESIDOC, etc. to be utilised as Sectoral Information Centres.

How to Participate in INFLIBNET ?

INFLIBNET being a national venture, any academic/Research and (R&D) institution can participate by

- Signing a Memorandum of Understanding (MOU)
- Adhering to standards prescribed by INFLIBNET
- Committing its resources for sharing

There will be a nominal charge for the services to ensure optimum use.

Membership of INFLIBNET

**Full Member*

- Institutions supported by University Grants Commission e.g. Universities, Deemed universities etc. are eligible to become Full Member.
- These members are eligible for receiving financial assistance for establishment of computerisation and networking facilities.

**Associate Member*

- Academic and R&D institutions not supported by UGC are eligible for Associate Membership.
- These members have to find the own resources for establishing facilities for computerisation and networking.

Full as well as Associate members can take advantage of all the facilities and services provided by INFLIBNET based on the Memorandum of Understanding (MOU)

Funding for INFLIBNET

Ministry of Human Resource Development (MHRD), Government of India has recently approved the programme and given permission to establish INFLIBNET Centre to execute INFLIBNET programme of the University Grants Commission.

The Centre for this programme has become an inter-university centre under section 12 [CCC] of the Act of the University Grants Commission and registered as an autonomous society in May, 1996 at Ahmedabad.

Total funding for this programme and for the centre is provided by University Grants Commission.

Governance body of INFLIBNET

INFLIBNET Centre is governed by a council, which is a body consisting of all members of Governing Body and members representing various sponsoring bodies viz. University

Grants Commission, All India Council of Technical Research, National Library, Universities and other centres working in the field. The council meets normally once a year. The council is represented by the Governing Board.

The affairs of the centre are managed, administered, directed and controlled by the Governing Board. The Governing Board consists of a Distinguished Academician and eminent personalities from the field of education and the experts in the field.

The day-to-day functioning of Centre is managed by the Director of Centre, who is also Member-Secretary of the Council and the Governing Board.

6.9 LUCKLIBNET

It is a Cooperative Venture of the Library and Information Personnel of the Special Libraries and Information Centres of Lucknow (LUSLIC) in the form of a Consortium.

LUSLIC strives to have qualitative cooperation among Libraries and Information Centres of Lucknow for a Productive and User Friendly Information Service to the Scientific Community of the Country in General and intellectuals and Professionals of the City.

Services/Activities

- Resource Sharing (ILL)
- Reprographic Service
- Union Catalogue of Serials
- Seminars/ Symposia

Aims and Objectives

Both academic and research activities are as dependent on nascent scientific & technical literature as they are on various raw materials, equipment and new methodologies. There is always an increasing demand for published literature, which also contains results of experiments. Periodicals, known variously as bulletins, journals, magazines, serials, transactions etc., published weekly, monthly, bimonthly, and quarterly or annually, may be designated as the most frequently used items among all reading materials available in any special library. In truth, they form the heart of the most specialized collections in all research libraries. Today in many scientific and technical libraries the greater part of budgetary allocation is consumed by subscription to periodicals and very negligible amount is left for books and other reading materials. Barring a few, the majority of them are very expensive; the more specialized the periodical the higher is the cost. Resource sharing by pooling literature held in various libraries has been accepted as a viable alternative to cater to the unsatiated demand of the patrons.

Formation of LUSLIC

LUSLIC - a local network of special libraries of Lucknow came into being in 1983 with its prime motto of

(i) Resource sharing
(ii) Optimum use of funds.

With an aim to provide information of the availability of journals in each Library for resource sharing, it was initially decided to compile a collective Union catalogue of the serial holdings of each library and publish it for the use of the Libraries and their users. This exercise was carried out also with an objective to avoid any unnecessary duplication of journal subscription in member libraries.

Use of Union Catalogue as an important tool in Resource Sharing is increasing day by day, specially in view of–

(a) the limited library budgets
(b) annual price-rise of foreign periodicals
(c) instability of Indian currency as against the foreign currencies, and
(d) demand of new periodicals for new frontier areas.

In this backdrop, the members of the LUSLIC took the decision to bring out a Union Catalogue to meet the aforesaid challenges. LUSLIC succeeded in providing a reference tool, in the form of a **'Union Catalogue of Periodicals'**, which would lead its participating libraries to get the right document from other libraries.

The first **"Union Catalogue of Current Periodicals in LUSLIC Libraries"** published in 1987 could provide locational information of 2011 learned periodicals available in 14 member libraries. Besides this, the Union Catalogue also helped the librarians and information scientists to identify avoidable duplication in subscription lists.

Considering the continuous changes in the periodical holdings of libraries revised **second edition** of the Union Catalogue was published in 1995. Meanwhile a good number of new and existing libraries have joined the LUSLIC forum. Their total holdings of periodicals encompass the various fields of science, technology, social sciences & humanities.

At present, the total number of Member Libraries of LUSLIC has reached Twenty, which include the libraries of Lucknow University, King George's Medical University, Sanjay Gandhi Post Graduate Institute of Medical Sciences, Industrial Toxicology Research Center, National Botanical Research Institute , Central Institute of Medicinal and Aromatic Plants, Birbal Sahni Institute of Paleobotany, Indian Council of Philosophical Research, Research Designs and Standards Organization, National Bureau of Fish Genetic Research, Institute of Engineering and Technology, Indian Institute of Sugarcane Research , Pradeshiya Investment Corporation of U.P., Hindustan Aeronautics Limited, Animal Husbandry Directorate, Giri Institute of Development Studies, National Research Laboratory for the Conservation of Cultural Property and Bankers Institute of Rural Development. **Central Drug Research Institute** functions as the Nodal Centre of the consortium and houses its secretariat.

The third edition of the Union Catalogue was published in 2000. This edition of Union Catalogue provided access to the literature published in periodicals, which are subscribed by 27 libraries (eighteen full-fledged Special Libraries and nine Departmental Libraries of Lucknow University) exposing a wealth of information of the periodical literature and its availability to interested readers, and also to the library and information specialists in Lucknow and outside. Entries in this catalogue are alphabetically arranged by the title of each periodical in the following order (i) serial number (ii) title (iii) country of origin (iv) periodicity and (v) abbreviated name(s) of libraries. Unlike its previous edition this union catalogue includes the holdings data with additional information like (a) the commencement (both volume and year) and (b) cessation (both volume and year) of the periodical in a particular library.

LUSLIC has launched its website under the domain name, LUCKLIBNET which provides the Union Catalogue of Periodicals (On Line) and gives information regarding each Member Library on the INTERNET. Apart from providing brief description of services and activities of member libraries, this online version of the Union catalogue provides search facility by name of the journal and member library name. The search output provides name of the libraries where a particular journal is available and the period of its back volume availability. Complete holding of each member library can also be obtained through Library-wise search option. As far as possible, up-to-date data has been incorporated in the Union catalogue. However, there are some member libraries who have not provided latest data. The data of these libraries will be incorporated as and when received.

6.10 STATUS OF LIBRARY NETWORKS IN INDIA

AS ON 2005.

Name of Networks	*Year of Starting*	*No. of Participating Libraries*	*Database and Activities*
ADINET	1994	9	Database on • Current periodicals • Library holdings • Training programmes
BALNET	1995	100	Database on • Computer and Software • Contents of Indian periodicals CD-ROM database searching On-line Union Catalogue of Periodicals Searching of Foreign database Software for OPAC
BONET	1992	17	On-line services • document delivery • access to foreign databases • catalogue of books & journals • catalogue of preprints/reprints

(Contd.)

			Other Services • Inter-library lending of books and periodicals • IRS • Consultation on standards
CALIBNET	1992	10	• Access to Internet and knight – Ridder (Dialog) • CD-ROM Database searching • On-line Search • IRS
DELNET	1988	878*165 Institute & 635 Library*15 States & 5 SAARC countries	Online Services • Inter Library Loan • Reprographic Service • Union Catalogue of the Serials • Seminars/ Symposia organization
INFLIBNET	1991	800	Database on • Books (6.5 Lakh) progress records; 50000 validated • Thesis/Dissertations (65,000 records) contents with abstracts (COPSAT) service • Periodicals Holdings
MALIBNET	1993	15	Database on • Periodicals Holdings (30,000 records of 60 libraries • Current Serials of 50 libraries • Journal contents (100,000 records) from member libraries • Automotive engineering (4,500 records) Access to Internet and Knight- Rider (Dialog) databaseCD-ROM database searching
MYLIBNET	1994	116	On-line Search • Books • Journals
LUCLIBNET	2000	27	Database on • Inter Library Loan • Reprographic Services • Union Catalogue of the Serials • Seminars/Symposia Organisations

During the recent period quite a large number of libraries and information centers are forming networks. The advent of computer networking as an accepted part of the library and information infrastructure has a very significant impact on the way in which library and information systems are perceived. India is thus on the threshold to a new era of computer communication networks both for general purposes and for library and information purposes.

*# Note: We are very much grateful to the following web sources, because we have taken a great help from them in the production and re-production of information in this chapter.

inflibnet.ac.in; btisnet.nic.in; mylibnet.org; inflibnet.ac.in, delnet.org, calibnet.org; alibnet.org; elnet.nic.in; indonet.net; lucklibnet.com ; ugc.ac.in; home.nic.in; ernet.in; unesco.org , infolibrarian.com, informindia.co.in, libraryworld.net, info.com/ librarySoftware, library.geac.com, librarysoftwares.net.

REFERENCES

1. Aswal, RS, ed. – Information Networks in India, New Delhi: Ess Ess Publication, 2003.
2. Baruah, A – Computer Networking in Libraries, Delhi; Kalpaz, 2002.
3. Desikan, RS and Muthuswamy, R – Configuring a Local Area Network System for a Technical Information Center: A Case Study, *IN* AGLIS Journal, Vol. 8, No. 1-4, 1991.
4. Elashami, AM – Networking CD-ROMs: The Decision Makers Guide to Local Area Network solutions, New York: American Library Association, 1996.
5. Jebaraj, Franklin David and Devadoss, Fredrick Robin – Library and Information Networks in India, *IN* Library Philosophy and Practice, Vol. 6, No. 2 (Spring 2004).
6. Lahiri, A ed. – Library Automation: The Real Crunch, NISSAT Newsletter Vol. 9; No. 2, 1990. (URL http://www.dsir.nic.in/pubs/itt/nnl9002/nnl9002.pdf)
7. Lucas, A and Nevallo, A ed. – Encyclopedia of Information Systems and Services, Detroit : Gale Research, 1990.
8. Malwad, NM *et.al.*, ed. – Digital Libraries: Dynamic Storehouse of Digitized Information: 15th Annual Convention and Conference 18-20 January, 1996, Bangalore: New Age International Publishers, 1996.
9. Murthy, SS *et.al.*, ed. – Bibliographic Databases and Networks : Proceedings of the International Conference 1989/organized by DESIDOC, New Delhi : Tata McGraw Hill, 1990.
10. Tripathi, SM – Documentation and Information Services and Networks, Vol. 2. Information Systems and Networks, Agra : Y.K. Publishers, 1997.

CHAPTER 7

INTERNET AND LIBRARIES

To sent or receive data within a matter of seconds to someone placed beyond the Pacific was unthinkable before the advent of the Internet. The Internet represents the transformation and evolution of the entire information age. It is due to these factors that people all over the globe have recognized the Internet as their latest development tool. Internet is making a major impact on the IT industry. Major companies like Microsoft, AT &T, Intel and IBM have networked their business strategy vis-a-vis the Internet.

Internet is extremely flexible, and is used to create everything from simple employee directories (much cheaper than printing 1000 copies) to complex database and Groupware applications.

7.1 DEFINITION

Internet is an inter-connection between several computers of different types belonging to various networks all over the globe. It is a network of networks.

In simple words, the Internet is the global association of computers that carries data and makes the exchange of Information possible.

The FNC agrees that the following language reflects our definition of the term "Internet" Internet refers to the global information system that -

---

(i) is logically linked together by a globally unique address space based on the Internet Protocol (IP) or its subsequent extensions/follow-one;

(ii) is able to support communications using the Transmission Control Protocol/ Internet Protocol (TCP?IP) suite or its subsequent extensions/follow-ons, and/or other IP-compatible protocols;

(iii) provides, uses or makes accessible, either publicly or privately, high level services layered on the communications and related infrastructure described herein.

7.2 ADVANTAGES

(a) As a Network
Organisations can use the Internet to link their offices and employees, tuning the Internet into a virtual private network.

(b) As a Medium
The Internet serves as a communication channel for anybody dealing with product marketing to corporate communications.

(c) As a Market
The Internet is vast virtual market place where you can advertise and even order products from the market.

(d) As a Transaction Platform
The Internet allows you to complete you business transactions in the market place, i.e. you complete your financial transactions online while linked directly to your suppliers, customers or financial institutions.
The Internet is an information super-highway and has compressed the world into a cyber colony.

7.3 FUNCTIONALITY OF THE INTERNET

The Internet has more than a million computers attached to it, from which arises the need of a proper addressing system for communications. The system of addressing is called the Internet Protocol (IP) addressing system. Each computer on the network is called a host, and has a name and a number that identifies it. The IP addressing systems uses:

- Letter Addressing System
- Number Addressing System

7.3.1 LETTER ADDRESSING SYSTEM

The last three letters of the address are important because they provide information about the kind of organization to which the address belongs.

Some of the abbreviations used are listed below:

Abbreviations	*Represent*
com	Commercial Organisation
edu	Educational Institutions
gov	Government Departments
int	International Organisations
mil	Military Sites
net	Networking Organisations

org	Professional Societies
nic	National Information Centre

The Letter Addressing System also uses country codes comprising two letters e.g.

in	India
ca	Canada
au	Australia

This Letter Addressing System is called Domain Naming Systems (DNS).

7.3.2 NUMBER ADDRESSING SYSTEM

A numeric address has four parts and is referred to as a dated quad. For example, 21, 122, 197, 222. This is also known as IP address. Each number in the dated quad, called an Octel, can not exceed 255. Internet being a packet switching network, converting it into small packets transmits data. The software that is responsible for managing the Internet function efficiently is TCP/IP, which stands for Transmission Control Protocol/ Internet Protocol.

Transmission Control Protocol (TCP)

It breaks up the data to be sent into the packets. It guarantees that any data sent to the destination, computer reaches it intact. It makes the process appear as if one computer is directly connected to the other providing what appears to be dedicated connection.

Internet Protocol (IP)

It is a set of connections used to pass packets from one host to another. It is responsible for routing the packets to a desired destination IP address. Packets are passed using three kinds of mechanisms

i. Bridges
ii. Routers
iii. Gateways

Accessing Internet

Proper access to the Internet depends on two things, namely, the user's interface connection and the installed browser. Different networks provide different kinds of services and connections. The types of connection chosen by the user will depend on the purpose for which the user intends to use the Internet.

Dedicated Access

A dedicated connection allows the user's computer to remain connected to the Internet 24 hours a day. It is a direct link to the Internet. Routers pass on the data to Internet backbones.

A Router is used to transmit data from one network to another. Backbones are high speed phone lines that move data to and from mid-level servers. These servers pass on the data to local networks.

Dial up Access

IP Accounts

When the user needs to access the Internet through a service provider, the user can have two kinds of accounts-SLIP accounts and PPP accounts, collectively known as IP accounts. A service provider has direct access to the Internet and provides Internet services to other users. The service provider assigns addresses to the users. Both SLIP (Serial Line Internet Protocol) and PPP (Point-to-Point Protocol) connections are similar to a dedicated line, though PPP connections are faster than SLIP connections. With an IP address, the computer appears to be a node on the network like a dedicated account. The software that the user uses on the machine is downloaded on the user's machine and not on the service provider.

Shell Accounts

With a shell account, the user can access the Internet for a fixed number of hours and is required to pay a monthly or an annual tariff for the service provider. A shell account holder can only view text and not graphics. With this kind of a system, the computer is not actually a part of the Internet and hence the user does not have any IP address.

Internet Requirements

To connect the Internet, the user needs a computer with communications software such as Telix, Procom Plus or PCP Plus to access the service provider. The hardware requirements to connect to the Internet are:

- An IBM compatible or higher PC< if the user intends to use the Internet for text.
- A PC-At 486 or higher with SVGA (Super Video Graphic Array) capabilities, if the user intends to use the GUI (Graphical User Interface) browser to navigate the Internet. A large capacity hard disk should be available to download the files.
- A modem that can handle at least 9600 bits per second (bps).

7.4 CONNECTIVITY WITH INTERNET

From AIT

AIT is connected to the Internet through AIII (Asian Internet Interconnection Initiative), World Net and NECTEC (National Electronics and Computer Technology Centre). In each division/outreach Centre the computers are connected to the campus backbone which in turn connects them to the Internet. All the Internet applications (netscape, telnet, etc.) can be used directly without making any additional changes.

Dial-up Connection

To access the net from other places, such as your home or hotel, you will need to have account with an Internet Service Provider (ISP) in that City. You will also need a modem, software for dialing the telephone number of you ISP and all necessary software such as a Web browser, telnet client, FTP client, etc. installed on your computer.

You can always access your ISP account by making a telephone call from anywhere in the world. This is of course, not at all recommended because of high telephone charges.

ISPs like IBM Net provide access to the net by dialing a local telephone number from more than 500 cities of the world.

Cyber-cafes or Internet Kiosks

Nowadays, cyber-cafes or Internet kiosks have come up in major cities. These allow anyone to use the Net for a charge. The charges for using a cyber-cafe vary from city to city and from one cyber-cafe to another cyber-café within the same city.

7.5 DOMAIN NAMES

Domain names provide a unique address to a computer on the Internet. These domain names are composed of alpha-numeric words.

A Domain Name is normally composed of three Top Level Domains (TLDs)

1ST LEVEL TLD

Domain names in many country use a two letter country designator. Domain Names in the United States have a "us" country designator, but it is not normally used, as most applicants prefer to register under the .com, .org, and .edu 1st TLD. These 1st TKDs do not require a country suffix, and for the purpose of clarity we call them 2nd level TLD. Increasing numbers of different nationals are now registering .com, .org, and .net domain names as their 1st TLD.

Some country abbreviations	
.au	Australia
.nz	New Zealand
.ca	Canada
.de	Germany
.uk	United Kingdom
.jp	Japan

2ND LEVEL TLD

The following designations are used:

.Com	Commercial organizations
.net	network provider
.org	non commercial organizations
.edu	educational institutions
.gov	government office (U.S. only)
.mil	U.S. Armed Forces

3RD LEVEL TLD

This indication of the individual business or person is the place to be creative. There can be up to 22 characters, using only letters, numbers or dashes.

7.6 WORLD WIDE WEB (WWW)

Popular www is a MOSAIC, a program developed by the National Centre for super computing applications at the University of Illinois. This program brings Web in the forefront of Internet tools. It introduces multimedia to a www with MOSAIC. The www or simply web is the most popular growing service on the Internet today. The Web actually born by late 1991 and by 1993 it began to really take off with the development of two slick browsers.

Components: There are two key components to the www:
Web Server
Web Browser

Web Server host Web documents, written in Hypertext Makeup Language (HTML_and transmit these over the Internet using Hypertext Transmission Protocol (HTTP), which operates on TCP/IP.

Web Browser is user interface software packages, which receive and display Web pages from the servers. Web browsers are available for numerous operating systems including Windows, OS/2, MacOS, and UNIX etc. Two popular browsers are:

Netscape
Internet Explorer

In addition to HTTP, www supports other access tools like e-mail, File Transfer Protocol (FTP), Gopher and Telnet, making it an all-in-one Internet User Interface.

Hypertext is the fundamental organizing concept of www. It refers to the embedding of links within an HTML page (web page) pointing to other documents. The linked documents could comprise text, images, graphics and charts, and audio-video clips. These documents need not exit in just one computer. They may be distributed among different Web servers at different geographical locations. HTML supports sophisticated information display capabilities and provides wide latitude to the information providers to control the page display format making up a document using HTML tags.

The growth in the variety of services and applications developed over the Web has been spectacular. These key Web services need mention here, viz. Forms-based query processing, Virtual Reality Modelling Language (VRML) and Java. WWW supports the search and retrieval of information from databases existing on Web servers using HTML based query forms. VRML has made it possible for viewing and manipulating 2D and 3D graphics. Java is emerging as a very important high level programming language for the WWW. Programs written in Java can be automatically transferred to the browser, where an embedded Java interpreter executes them.

WWW is an application system implemented on computers connected to the Internet, enabling multiple computers with disparate operating systems to communicate using HTML as their lingua franca. WWW has made the Internet today; WWW is the largest information resource of easily accessible web. The information sources around the world are getting inter-linked through Web pages and Web servers spread around the globe.

Number of organizations maintains an on-line catalogue of their publications over Internet/WWW could be searched using navigation tools. The users can select items of interest and click for further processing. Many publishers maintain the content pages of their journal on WWW. Such services can be effectively used for CAS/SDI services by the libraries, which are subscribing of the journals.

Universal resource locators on the Web like Yahoo and Lycos allow the users to enter a Web page under an appropriate category. This also enables the users of a particular category to see related home pages.

7.7 INTRANET, EXTRANET AND INTERNET

Intranet

A website used within the internal network of the company. Corporate intranets can facilitate communication and efficiency in the areas of sales, marketing, service, training, human resources, filing, administration, and corporate culture building. It may include message boards, mechanisms to share documentation, schedules/calendars.

Extranet

Similar to a corporate intranet, except an extranet allows for some external access. Extranets are often business-to-business communication tools that allow for an organization to share information with clients, customers, vendors, distributors, and partners. An order processing system can be an example of an extranet.

Both are used to improve business communication and information exchange for quicker turnaround time, decreased paper flow, increased productivity, and reduced costs.

The term "**intranet**" is somewhat misleading conceptually, because it invites a contrast to the term "Internet." The real contrast is with the World Wide Web—an important distinction, because "Internet" focuses on physical and technical networks, while the Web focuses on the set of content accessible on that physical and technical infrastructure.

The term "Intranet" coined by Amdahl Corporation in the summer of 1994 had the connotation of an internal Web rather than just an internal Internet. In fact, the term we used internally before this was the too-cumbersome "Enterprise-Wide Web."

In the early days, an intranet defined as "An infrastructure based on Internet standards and technologies that supports sharing of content within a limited and well-defined group." The "infrastructure" referred to the organizational and management infrastructure that created, managed, and shared the content. The only technical constraint was that the physical network be based on the Internetworking Protocol (IP).

You might notice that this definition encompasses what we call extranets today, because the defining factor is a "limited and well-defined group," and does not specify any official organizational affiliation. The Web, in contrast, is an unlimited group.

An intranet is a set of content shared by a well-defined group within a single organization. An extranet is a set of content shared by a well-defined group, but one that crosses enterprise boundaries.

As technical infrastructure becomes less of a barrier to accessing specific content, it becomes important to pay attention to how, or if, we want to restrict access. The terms "intranet" and "extranet," as imperfect as they are, provide us with conceptual and pragmatic tools for discussing to whom we want to make specific content available.

These terms may continue to evolve in meaning. For now, a set of content accessed by members of a single organization is an intranet, even if the information travels across the public Internet infrastructure.

7.8 COMMON TERMS AND ACRONYMS

The followings are most commonly used terms and acronyms which one would come across while using the net. A more detailed explanation of these can be found at any of the websites listed below:

1. Anonymous FTP

By using the word 'anonymous' as your user ID and your email address as the password when you login to an FTP site, you can bypass local security checks and gain limited access to public files on the remote computer. This type of access is available on most FTP sites, but not all.

2. Applet

A small Java program that can be embedded in an HTML page. Applets differ from full-fledged jave applications in that they are not allowed to access certain resources on the local computer, such as files and serial devices (modems, printers, etc.), and are prohibited from communicating with most other computers across a network. The current rule is that an applet can only make an Internet connection to the computer from which the applet was sent.

3. Arpanet (Advanced Research Projects Agency Network)

The precursor to the Internet. Developed in the late 60's and early 70's by the US Department of Defense as an experiment in wide-area-networking that would survive a nuclear war.

4. Bandwidth

How much stuff you can send through a connection. Usually measured in bits-per-second. A full page of English text is about 16000 bits. A fast modem can move about 15000 bits in one second. Full-motion full-screen video would require roughly 10,000,000 bits per second, depending on compression.

5. BBS (Bulletin Board System)

A computerized meeting and announcement system that allows people to carry on discussions, upload and download files, and make announcements without the people being connected to the computer at the same time. There are many thousands (millions) of BBS's around the world, most are very small, running on a single IBM clone PC with 1 or 2 phone lines. Some are very large and the line between a BBS and a system like CompuServe gets crossed at some point, but it is not clearly drown.

6. BITNET (Because It's Time NETwork or because It's There NETwork)

A network of educational sites separate from the Internet, but e-mail is freely exchanged between BITNET and the Internet. Listserves, the most popular form of e-mail discussion groups, originated on BITNET. BITNET machines are usually mainframes running the VMS operating system, and the network is probably the only international network that is shrinking.

7. Browser

A client program (software) that is used to look at various kinds of Internet resources.

8. CGI (Common Gateway Interface)

A set of rules that describe how a Web Server Communicates with another piece of software on the same machine, and how the other piece of software (the CGI program) talks to the web server. Any piece of software can be a CGI program if it handles input and output according to the CGI standard. Usually a CGI program is a small program that takes data from a web server and does something with it, like putting the content of a form into an e-mail message, or turning the data into a database query. You can often see that a CGI program is being used by seeing "cgi-bin" in a URL, but not always.

9. Client

A software program that is used to contact and obtain data from a Server software program on another computer, often across a great distance. Each client program is designed to work with one or more specific kinds of Server programs, and each Server requires a specific kind of client. A Web Browser is a specific kind of Client.

10. Domain Name

The unique name that identifies an Internet site. Domain Names always have 2 or more parts, separated by dots. The part on the left is the most specific, and the part on the right is the most general. A given machine may have more than one Domain Name but a given Domain Name points to only one machine. For example, the domain names:

Matisse.net
Mail.matisee.net
Workshop.matisse.net

Can all refer to the same machine, but each domain name can refer to no more than one machine. Usually, all of the machines of a given Network will have the same thing as the right-hand portion of their Domain Names. It is also possible for a Domain Name to exist but not be connected to an actual machine. This is often done so that a group or business can have an Internet e-mail address without having to establish a real Internet site. In these cases, some real Internet machine must handle the mail on behalf of the listed Domain Name.

11. FAQ

Acronym for Frequently Asked Questions. FAQs are widely available on the Internet and usually take the form of latrge, instructional text files. They are written on a wide variety of topics, and are usually the most up-to-date. Source for specialized information.

12. Finger

An Internet software tool for locating people on other Internet sites. Finger is also sometimes used to give access to non-personal information, but the most common use is to see if a person has an account at a particular Internet site. Many sites do not allow incoming Finger requests, but many do.

13. Fire Wall

A combination of hardware and software that separates a LAN into two or more parts for security purpose.

14. FTP (File Transfer Protocol)

A very common method of moving files between two Internet sites. FTP is a special way to login to another Internet site for the purposes for retrieving and or sending files. There are many Internet sites that have established publicly accessible repositories of material that can be obtained using FTP, by logging in using the account name anonymous, thus these sites are called anonymous FTP servers.

FTP stands for File Transfer Protocol. This is used for transferring files from one computer to another computer on the Internet.

15. Gateway

The technical meaning is a hardware or software set-up that translates between two dissimilar protocols, for example Prodigy has a gateway that translates between its internal, proprietary e-mail format and Internet e-mail. Another, sloppier meaning of gateway is to describe any mechanism for providing access to another system, e.g. AOL might be called a gateway to the Internet.

16. Gopher

A widely successful method of making menus of material available over the Internet. Gopher is a Client and Server style program, which requires that the user have a Gopher Client program. Although Gopher spread rapidly across the globe in only a couple of years, it has been largely supplanted by Hypertext, also known as WWW. There are still thousands of Gopher Servers on the Internet and we can expect they will remain for a while.

Gophers were more in use before WWW became popular. Unlike WWW, which has clickable words, graphics, music and video, the gophers could only have a directory sort of structure. It is basically a client and server style program.

To see the difference, please logon your rccsun or alphserv account by telnetting and type gopher at the prompt. You will then be able to see what gopher is. Please use arrow keys to move on a gopher file.

Gopher://peg/cwis.uci.edu:7000/

Shows a gopher server running on a non-standard port (the standard gopher port is 70).

The standard ports for some services are:

Service	Port
World Wide Web	80
Gopher	70
Telnet	23
FTP	21

17. Home Page (or Homepage)

Originally, the web page that your browser is set to use when it starts up. The more common meaning refers to the main web page for a business, organization, person or simply the main page out of a collection of web pages, e.g. "Check our so-and-so's new Home Page." Another sloppier use of the term refers to practically any web page as a "homepage", e.g. That website has 65 homepages and none of them are interesting.

18. Host

Any computer on a network that is a repository for services available to other computers on the network. It is quite common to have one host machine provide several services, such as WWW and USENET.

19. HTML (Hyper Text Markup Language)

The coding language used to create Hypertext documents for use on the World Wide Web. HTML looks a lot like old-fashioned typesetting code, where you surround a block of text with codes that indicate how it should appear, additionally; in HTML you can specify that a clock of text, or a word, is linked to another file on the Internet. HTML files are meant to be viewed using a World Wide Web Client Program, such as Netscape or Mosaic.

20. HTTP (Hyper Text Transport Protocol)

The protocol for moving hypertext files across the Internet. Requires a HTTP client program on one end, and an HTTP server program on the other end. HTTP is the most important protocol used in the WWW.

21. Hypertext

Generally, any text that contains links to other documents – words or phrases in the document that can be chosen by a reader and which cause another document to be retrieved and displayed.

22. Internet (Upper Case)

The vast collection of inter-connected networks that all use the TCP/IP protocols and that evolved from the ARPANET of the late 60's and early 70's.

23. Internet (Lower Case)

Any time you connect 2 or more networks together, you have an Internet- as in inter-national or inter-state.

24. InterNIC

Meaning Internet Information Center, InterNIC is the combined name for the providers of registration, information, and database services to the Internet. InterNIC is who you contact if you want to register a domain name on the Internet.

25. Interanet

A private network inside a company or organization that uses the same kinds of software that you would find on the public Internet, but that is only for internal use. As the Internet has become more popular many of the tools used on the Internet are being used in private networks, for example, many companies have web servers that are available only to employees.

26. IP Address (Internet Protocol Number)

Sometimes called a dotted quad. A unique number consisting of 4 parts separated by dots, e.g. 165.113.245.2 Every machine that is on the Internet has a unique IP number – if a machine does not have an IP number, it is not really on the Internet. Most machines also have one or more Domain Names that are easier for people to remember.

27. IRC (Internet Relay Chat)

Basically a huge multi-user live chat facility. There are a number of major IRC servers around the world which are linked to each other. Anyone can create a channel and anything that anyone types in a given channel is seen by all other in the channel. Private channels can create for multi-person conference calls.

28. ISP (Internet Service Provider)

An institution that provides access to the Internet in some form, usually for money.

29. Java

Java is a network-oriented programming language invented by Sub Microsystems that is specifically designed for writing programs that can be safely downloaded to your computer through the Internet and immediately run without fear of viruses or other harm to your computer or files. Using small Java programs (called "Applets"); Web pages can include functions such as animations, calculators, and other fancy tricks.

We can expect to see a huge variety of features added to the Web using Java, since you can write a Java program to do almost anything a regular computer program can do, and then include that Java program in a Web page.

30. MIME (Multipurpose Internet Mail Extensions)

The standard for attaching non-text files to standard Internet mail messages. Non-text files include graphics, spreadsheets, formatted word-processor documents, sound files, etc.

An e-mail program is said to be MIME compliant if it can both send and receive files using the MIME standard. When non-text files are sent using the MIME standard they are converted (encoded) into text- although the resulting text is not really readable.

Generally speaking the MIME standard is a way of specifying both the type of file being sent (e.g. a Quicktime™ video file), and the method that should be used to turn it back into its original form. Besides email software, the MIME standard is also universally used by Web Servers to identify the files they are sending to Web Clients, in this way new file formats can be accommodated simply by updating the Browsers' list of pairs of MIME-Types and appropriate software for handling each type.

31. Mirror

Generally speaking, "to mirror" is to maintain an exact copy of something. Probably the most common use of the term on the Internet refers to "mirror sites" which are web sites, or FTP sites that maintain exact copies of material originated at another location, usually in order to provide more widespread access to the resource. Another common use of the term 'mirror' refers to an arrangement where information is written to more than one hard disk simultaneously, so that if one disk fails, the computer keeps on working without losing anything.

32. Netscape

A www Browser and the name of a company. The Netscape browser was originally based on the Mosaic program developed at the National Center for Super Computing Applications (NCSA).

Netscape has grown in features rapidly and is widely recognized as the best and most popular web browser. Netscape Corporation also produces web server software.

Netscape provide major improvements in speed and interface over other browsers, and has also engendered debate by creating new elements for the HTML language used by Web pages- but the Netscape extensions to HTML are not universally supported.

The main author of Netscape, Mark Andreessen, was hired away from the NCSA by Jim Clark, and they founded a company called Mosaic Communications and soon changed the name to Netscape Communications Corporation.

33. Plug-in

A usually small piece of software that adds features to a larger piece of software. Common examples are plug-ins for the Netscape® browser and web server. Adobe Photoshop® also uses plug-ins.

The idea behind plug-in's is that a small piece of software is loaded into memory by the larger program, adding a new feature, and that users need only install the few plug-ins that they need, out of a much larger pool of possibilities. Plug-ins is usually created by people other than the publishers of the software the plug-in works with.

34. POP (Point of Presence, also Post Office Protocol)

Two commonly used meanings: Point of Presence and Post Office Protocol. A Point of Presence usually means a city or location where a network can be connected to, often with dial up phone lines. So if an Internet company says they will soon have a POP in Belgrade, it means that they will soon have local phone number in Belgrade and/or a place where leased lines can connect to their network. A second meaning, Post Office Protocol refers to the way e-mail software such as Eudora gets mail from a mail server. When you obtain a SLIP, PPP, or shell account you almost always get a POP account with it, and it is this POP account that you tell your e-mail software to use to get your mail.

35. Port: 3 Meanings

First and most generally, a place where information goes into or out of a computer, or both e.g. the serial post on a personal computer is where a modem would be connected.

On the Internet port often refers to a number that is part of a URL, appearing after a colon right after the domain name. Every service on an Internet server listens on a particular port number on that server. Most services have standard port numbers, e.g. Web servers normally listen on port 80. Services can also listen on non-standard ports, in which case the port number must be specified in a URL when accessing the server, so you might see a URL of the form.

36. PPP (Point to Point Protocol)

Most well known as a protocol that allows a computer to use a regular telephone line and a modem to make TCP/IP connections and thus be really and truly on the Internet.

37. Proxy Server

A proxy is a special server that typically runs in conjunction with firewall software. The proxy server waits for a request from inside the firewall, forwards the request to the remote server outside the firewall, reads the response, then sends the response back to the client.

38. RFC (Request for Comments)

The name of the result and the process for creating a standard on the Internet. New standards are proposed and published on line, as a Request For Comments. The Internet Engineering Task Force is a consensus-building body that facilitates discussion, and eventually a new standard is established, but the reference number/name for the standard retains the acronym RFC, e.g. the official standard for e-mail is REC 822.

39. Server

A computer, or a software package, that provides a specific kind of service to client software running on other computers. The term can refer to a particular piece of software, such as a WWW server, or to the machine on which the software is running, e.g. our mail server is down today, that's why e-mail is not getting out. A single server machine could have several different server software packages running on it, thus providing many different servers to clients on the network.

40. SLIP (Serial Line Internet Protocol)

A standard for using a regular telephone line (a serial line) and a modem to connect a computer as a real Internet site. SLIP is gradually being replaced by PPP.

41. SMTP (Simple Mail Transport Protocol)

The main protocol used to send electronic mail on the Internet.
SMTP consists of a set of rules for how a program sending mail and a program receiving mail should interact.

Almost all Internet e-mail is sent and received by clients and servers using SMTP, thus if one wanted to set up an e-mail server on the Internet one would look for e-mail server software that supports SMTP.

42. Sysop (System Operator)

Anyone responsible for the physical operations of a computer system or network resource. A System Administrator decides how often backups and maintenance should be performed and the System Operator performs those tasks.

43. TCP/IP (Transmission Control Protocol/Internet Protocol)

This is the suite of protocols that defines the Internet. Originally designed for theUNIX operating System, TCP/IP software is now available for every major kind of computer operating system. To be truly on the Internet, your computer must have TCP/IP software.

44. Terminal

A device that allows you to send commands to a computer somewhere else. At a minimum, this usually means a keyboard and display screen and some simple circuitry. Usually you will use terminal software in a personal computer- software pretends to be (emulates) a physical terminal and allows you to types commands to a computer somewhere else.

45. UNIX

A computer operating system (the basic software running on a computer, underneath things like word processors and spreadsheets). UNIX is designed to be used by many people at the same time (it is multi-user) and has TCP/IP build-in. It is the most common operating system for servers on the Internet.

46. URL (Uniform Resource Locator)

The standard way to give the address of any resource on the Internet that is part of the World Wide Web (WWW). A URL looks like this:

http://www.matisse.net/seminars/html

The most common way to use a URL is to enter into a WWW browser program, such as Netscape, or Lynx.

47. USENET

A world wide system of discussion groups, with comments passed among hundreds of thousands of machines. Not all USENET machines are on the Internet, maybe half. USENET is completely decentralized, with over 10,000 discussion areas, called newsgroups.

48. WWW (World Wide Web)

First meaning , loosely used : the whole constellation of resources that can be accessed using Gopher, FTP, HTTP, telnet, USENET, WAIS, and some other tools.

Second, the universe of hypertext servers (HTTP servers) which are the servers that allows text, graphics, sound files, etc. to be mixed together.

Web Sites

The Internet language dictionary, <http://www.netlingo.com>
Cnet's Glossary, <http://www.cnet.com>
Glossary.com: Computing and the Internet <http://www.glossary.com>
Learn the Net: An Internet Guide and Tutorial, <http://www.learnthenet.com>

49. Telnet

Telnet is a program that lets you use the power of the Internet to connect to databases, library catalogues, and other information resources around the world. It allows a user to connect to a remote computer to use applications.

- To access alphaserv from the netscape window, type telnet://rccsun.ait.ac.th or telnet://aphaserv.ait.ac.th, you can then access your account by supplying username and password. This way you can access any telnet site from netscape window.

50. E-mail

There is a lot of way to use the Internet. When you visit a Website, you are using the Internet. If you go to an FTP site, you are also using the Internet. But the most popular use of the Internet- by far- is e-mail. e-mail is just like regular mail, except instead of receiving a letter in you mailbox at your house, you receive email in an electronic mailbox on your computer.

Electronic mail allows almost instantaneous exchange of letters, messages and files with people in many countries of the world. One of the most powerful features of email is electronic mailing lists-like minded people sharing their expertise.

The following should serve as basic guidelines:

- Always assume that mail on the Internet is not secure. Or it is just like a postcard which can be read by others.
- If you are forwarding or re-posting a message, do not change the wording.
- It is a good practice to include a short signature file at the end of each e-mail message.
- Always try to know whom you are sending the message. Many offices just have one e-mail account and their e-mail is not necessarily read by the person whom you send.
- Never send an e-mail completely in UPPERCASE, it looks like as if you are shouting.
- Try to limit line length to fewer than 65 characters and end a line with carriage return.

7.9 IMPACT OF INTERNET ON LIBRARIES

While the internet revolution is leading to big changes for librarians all over the world, it is still in its infant stage in the Indian libraries. Though, there are a very few technocrats who have just jumped on the bandwagon to make everything computerized and networked yet a large number of librarians have not kept pace with the technology. They are silent spectator of whatever happens and want someone else to do for them. It should be realized that Internet will help libraries in following areas:

(i) By designing clearly organized, easily accessible and well published web sites, the librarians can extend the traditional librarianship to the use of information technology and series a leadership role in both fields.
(ii) The libraries can initiate Bulletin Board Service, which gives complete information regarding services, products, and various events organized by them.
(iii) Ready reference service can be provided with greater speed and in much shorter time.
(iv) Books and journals can be ordered online, technical processing of the documents too can be done without much effort.
(v) e-mail services can be used for delivering information to the users and communicating with the fellow information professionals.
(vi) E-SDI services can be used for delivering information professionals.
(vii) Access to various databases and OPAC of other libraries located in remote areas can be provided.

7.10 INTERNET LIBRARIES

A lot of libraries provide information resources on the Internet ranging from online public access catalogs to specialized databases and unique archival resources. While some of these libraries offer little more than basic information for their users and a link to their catalogs, other make available specialized services or databases that will be of interest to Internet users and not just local library users. Few of them named below:

Name of Library/Sponsor
General

1. AFIT Academic Library Air Force Institute of Technology
2. Air University Library
3. AISO Defense Language Institute Library
4. Center for Electronic Records National Archives and Records Administration (NARA)
5. CRREL Library Cold Regions Research and Engineering Laboratory
6. Daedalus: The Aeromedical Library OnlineBrooks Air Force Base
7. Dudley Knox LibraryNaval Postgraduate School
8. EPA National Online Library SystemEnvironmental Protection Agency
9. Federal Bureau of Prisons Library
10. Fermilab Information Resources LibraryFermi National Accelerator Laboratory
11. General Services Administration Library Catalog

12. GOVDDC-L
13. Homer e. Newell Memorial LibraryGoddard Space Flight Center
14. LLNL Library ServicesLawrence Livermore National Laboratory
15. Los Alamos LibraryLos Alamos National Laboratory
16. Lunar and Planetary Institute Library
17. Major Shared Resources Center Technical LibraryAeronautical Systems Center
18. The Marine Corps University Libraries
19. NASA Langley Research Center LibraryLaRC
20. National Defense University Library
21. National Institute for Literacy Library
22. National Radio Astronomy Observatory Library- NRAO
23. Navy Department Library
24. NCAR LibraryNational Center for Atmospheric Research
25. NCI Scientific LibraryFrederick Cancer Research and Development Center
26. NIEHS LibraryNational Institute of Environmental Health Sciences
27. NIH Library Online
28. Nimitz LibraryNaval Academy Library
29. NIST Virtual LibraryNational Institute of Standards and Technology Library
30. NDAA Seattle Regional LibraryNational Oceanic and Atmospheric Administration, LIS Division
31. Northwest and Alaska Fisheries Science Centers Library
32. NRL Library InfoWebNaval Research Laboratory
33. Phillips Site Technical LibraryKirtland Air Force Base, Phillips Laboratory Library
34. Ralph J. Bunche LibraryDepartment of State Library
35. Research Library at Brookhaven National Laboratory
36. Sandia National Laboratories Technical Library
37. SILIBS-L
38. Smithsonian Institution Libraries
39. U.S. Army Engineer Waterways Experiment Station Research Library-Waterways Experiment Station
40. United States Naval Observatory Library -Naval Observatory
41. Wallops Technical Library- Goddard Space Flight Center. Wallops Technical Library
42. Wright Net : Library and STINFOAir Force Research Laboratory Library
43. Basic Depository Library DocumentsUniversity of Denver Library GPO
44. Claitor's GPO Sales Product Catalog File Master IndexClaitor's Law Book
45. Depository Library Council
46. Documents Data Miner

47. Electronic Books and Pamphlets, Government DocumentsUniversity of Buffalo Library
48. Enhanced Shipping List Service State University of New York at Buffalo Library
49. Federal Depository Libraries Joint Committee on Printing
50. Federal Depository Library Program Administration Superintendent of Documents
51. DODORT Cataloging Committee Government Document Round Table Cataloging Committee
52. Godort Handout ExchangeGovernment Document Round Table, University of Michigan, Documents Center
53. Government Information Technology Committee/GODORT,GITCO
54. Government Publications Network/Bernan Associates
55. Inter-Association Working Group on Government Information Policy/IAWG
56. Map Room FTP Files/Colorado School of Mines Library
57. Monthly Catalog of Publications (MOCAT)/Government Printing Office, Superintendent of Documents
58. Needs and Offers List/University of the South Library
59. Pathway Services Browse Electronic Titles: The Virtual Depository/Government Printing Office, Superintendent of Documents
60. Resources of Use to Government Documents Librarians/Depository Library Council, University of California, Berkeley Library
61. Superintendent of Documents/GPO
62. U.S. Government Printing Office/ GPO
63. Uncle Sam Migrating Government Publications/ University of Memphis Library

National

1. Catalogs (Library of Congress)/LC
2. Library of Congress MARVEL/LC
3. National Agricultural Library /NAL
4. National Archives and Records Administration/ NARA
5. National Commission on Libraries and Information Science/ NCLIS
6. National Library of Education/NLE
7. National Library of Medicine/ NLM

Other Libraries

1. AcqWeb
2. American Society of Indexers home page
3. Building Digital Libraries on the Web

4. Celebrate Libraries
5. Christian Classics Ethereal Library
6. Librarian Portal
7. Internet Public Library
8. Internet Resources for Cataloguing
9. Librarie's Professional Resources
10. Library Job Hunting
11. Library Resource List
12. National Archives and Records Administration
13. OCLC Online Computer Library Center
14. A Plethora of Web Sites : The Librarian's Meta List
15. School Libraries on the Web
16. Smithsonian Institution Libraries
17. Understanding Call Numbers
18. WWW Library Directory
19. The Perry Castafieda Library Map Collection
20. Rare map Collection at the Hargrett Library

REFERENCES

1. Baruah, A – Computer Networking in Libraries, Delhi; Kalpaz, 2002.
2. Desikan, RS and Muthuswamy, R – Configuring a Local Area Network System for a Technical Information Center: A Case Study, *IN* AGLIS Journal, vol. 8, No. 1-4, 1991.
3. Elashami, AM – Networking CD-ROMs: The Decision Makers Guide to Local Area Network Solutions, New York: American Library Association, 1996.
4. Haung, Samuel, T – Modern Library Technology and Reference Services, N.Y.: Haworth Press, 1993.
5. Lucas, A and Nevallo, A ed. – Encyclopedia of Information Systems and Services, Detroit: Gale Research, 1990.
6. Murthy, SS et.al. ed. – Bibliographic Databases and Networks: Proceedings of the International Conference 1989/organized by DESIDOC, New Delhi: Tata McGraw Hill, 1990.
7. Tripathi, SM – Documentation and Information Services and Networks, Vol. 2. Information Systems and Networks, Agra: Y.K. Publishers, 1997.
8. Valauskas, Edward, J and John, Nancy, R ed. – Internet Initiative: Libraries Providing Internet Services and How They Plan Pay and Manage, N.Y.: American Library Association, 1995.
9. Websites: inflibnet.ac.in ; btisnet.nic.in; mylibnet.org; calibnet.org; alibnet.org; elnet.nic.in; indonet.net; lucklibnet.com ; ugc.ac.in; home.nic.in; ernet.in; unesco.org

CHAPTER 8

DIGITAL AND VIRTUAL LIBRARIES

The advancement in Electronic Library is called Digital Library. Electronic library contains digitized information as well as print-based publication but digital library contains information only in digital form. In both the libraries users can communicate with it over a telephone link or a co-axial or a fibre optic cable.

8.1 CONCEPT OF DIGITAL LIBRARY

Digital Libraries does not mean "libraries" in the classical sense, but a network of multimedia systems. A typical digital library is a media server (group of inter linked workstations) connected to high-speed networks. Unlike traditional libraries, digital libraries don't reside building. Digital information is based on just two distinct states. The digital evolution is bounded on the characteristics of digital information. The digital information is manipulate-able, network-able, dense, compressible and impartial. In addition to traditional text based information data accessible through the digital library system includes non-text information (Photographs, drawings, illustration etc.); streams of numeric data, satellite information, cosmological data) digitized sound and moving, visual images. Image information stored in digital format manipulates automatically at high speed.

A Digital Library is visualized as a server which is having linkage to various other forms. A Digital Library has mainly three characteristics:

- Storage in digital form i.e. works such as books, magazines, newspapers; records, videos etc. are to be stored in digital format.
- Readers no longer need to come to a library; they use electronic methods to have material delivered to them.
- Material is always copied from the master version of the work in the electronic library.

The term *digital and electronic library* are being used synonymously which is not the exact case; "**Electronic library** is widespread use of electronic media for the storage, retrieval and delivery of information. Electronic library may not necessarily be networked, but would certain digitized information along with print based publications." All the material in libraries can not be digitized immediately; the priority may be given to the old stock material most frequently used. Therefore, the material not so frequently used remains in the libraries in the printed form and the existing conventional form of libraries co-exist with electronic library.

The advantage of having library material available in digital form is three folds:

- The data occupies less space and can be replicated easily and made sure electronically.
- The data can be made immediately available through communication networks like INTERNET to anyone, anywhere.
- Provides enormous search speed and facility. The promise of the digital library is the promise of a great cost reduction while providing great increase in data availability and accessible.

8.2 DEFINITION

- **Digital library** can be defined as "Computer based information system for acquiring, storing, organizing, searching, distributing and displaying digital materials for end of access, designed and constructed as to be capable of attaching or being attached to a network."

It tends to cover following facts:

- The digital library is not a single entity;
- The digital library requires technology to link the resources of many such collections;
- The linkage between the many digital libraries and information centre are transparent to the end-users;
- Universal access to digital libraries and information services is a goal;
- Digital library collections are not limited to document surrogates: they extend to digital artefacts that can not be represented or distributed imprinted format.
- **Yerkey** defined: "Digital libraries as electronic libraries in which large number of geographically distributed users can access the content of large and diverse repositories of electronic objects. Electronic objects include networked text, images, maps, sounds, videos and scientific business and government data sets."
- A digital library is a global virtual library: "the library of thousands of networked electronic libraries" as defined by **Ray. R. Iarson**, CSIR Electronic Library Project Group. University of California, Berkeley, 1994.

- Digital libraries are "system providing users with coherent access to a very large organized repository of information and knowledge" as defined by **the working group of the U.S. Govt. Information Infrastructure Technology and Applications.**

8.3 PURPOSE AND OBJECTIVES

- To expedite the systematic development of the means to collect, store and organize information and knowledge in digital form;
- To provide the economical and efficient delivery of information to all;
- To strengthen communication and collaboration between and among there search business, government and educational communities;
- To take international role in the generation and dissemination of knowledge;
- To distribute to the lifelong learning opportunities of people.

8.4 STORAGE AND RETRIEVAL OF INFORMATION

8.4.1 STORAGE OF INFORMATION

We are in early stage of a transition from a print based to a digital society. Digital information can be stored on any medium that is able to represent binary digit 0 & 1. Conversion from the conventional storage to digitized format requires discrete analysis as the primary function based on user electronic storage and retrieval system could be defined and a target concept could be developed.

Some of the common digitized storage media that are presently used world over is: Hyper books, CD-ROM, Multimedia.

Hyper Books

Hyper Books are electronic books defined on the basis of the paper back metaphor.

The advantages of hyper books are:

- It can be shared by user in different geographical locations
- It is quick, accurate, easy to locate by using searching and browsing mechanism
- Binding for preservation and shelf maintenance do not exist

Hyper Books contain text and geographical images. Geographical object is always visible and appears in the text as in paper book. The feature of the text is that it contains embedded links i.e. active text that is connected to other parts of the book.

CD-ROM

The first product in evolutionary optical storage information is CD-ROM. It is permanent optical based storage device. That in conjunction with an associated drive becomes a powerful peripheral for the PC. Its only drawback is that the end user can not put his own information on it. The advantages of storing data on CD are:

- High storage capacity (600 MB)
- Long life
- Easily transportable
- Low cost
- Reliable medium
- Less shelf space
- No head crash
- Random access
- Low error rate

The advantage that made CD-ROM practically attractive in today's competing information environment are:

(a) **Multimedia** – The ability to deliver unlimited end users access to over 600 MB information delivered using ordinary post means; it can be used for text, graphics, data, audio & video in one simple purchase.

(b) **Multilingual** – Sophisticated CD-ROM systems today allow the end users to select the operating language at choice and change it on the fly.

The CD-ROM being taken over by yet another media called *DVD (Digital Video Disks)*, a single disk which can hold database of 10 CD-ROMs.

8.4.2 RETRIEVAL OF INFORMATION

The following stages are important in retrieval of information:

- The analysis of search question.
- The translation of the question into the indexing language of the system.
- The formation of the search strategy.

In addition, a lot of service problems occur such as, how to provide copies of documents, how to display them, how to manage search and retrieval, how to protect, copyright and how to manage loans.

To avoid these problems, electronic environment interface design is a very important issue. There are various ways for example –

- **Plain Text Interface**: Electronic documents are presented as plain text without images or other multimedia elements.

- **Image based interface**: The material is presented in image form of only some relevant parts.
- **Hypermedia based interface**: Electronic documents are presented following the paper book metaphor and the digital library design reproduces the main features of the physical library.

The catchwords in the retrieval systems are online, Internet etc.:

- **Online:** Online makes information available in different formats. It is a means of constant access to database around the world from any location using an inexpensive telecom link and PC terminals.
- **Internet:** The Internet is a co-operative computers network of networks that links libraries schools, governments, corporations, individuals and other to each other and to vase information resources. Internet can be used to send and receive electronic messages, to contact and search other computers. The Internet is an open network; anyone or any group is welcome to use it as long as that person or group has a terminal or a computer with the correct software and the ability to pay the cost. This INTERNET is heading a new fully wired digital society.

8.5 DIGITAL INFORMATION DELIVERY

A document delivery system comprises just there components—a document store or archive (sending station), a means of delivery, i.e. transmission telecom system, a receiving station.

a. **Document store or archive**: An archive can be a basic minimal storage telecopy, a PC with a data communication interface to either a wide area network or a local area network or a mainframe with data communication hardware & software.
b. **Communication**: Insertion of digital representation of documents into telecommunications networks for delivery required one or more communications modules in the documents archive.
c. **The documents receiving station**: A desktop computer with a suitable operator interface (keyboard, screen, and pointer), 300 pixels per inch printer and the telecom interface necessary to receive.

8.6 ADVANTAGES

Electronic information potentially easy to access, use, manipulate and printed in wide variety of formats. It is cheaper to store which reduces demands on libraries for additional 'Shelf' or storage space. Obsolescence and technological advancements are however, issues, which must be considered in evaluating the economics of electronic storage.

- More timely information
- Easier feedback via linked community
- More convenient access

- Local copying on demand
- Potential for creative use of hypertext links and multimedia features.
- Lower apparent cost to parent organization
- Incentive to develop new network tools
- Cost appears to decline.

8.7 LIMITATIONS

- Lack of screening or validation
- Lack of quality control and editing standards
- Lack of preservation "of best in class"
- Difficulty in knowing and locating everything that is available and differentiating valuable from useless information
- Job loss for traditional publishers and librarians
- Lack of preservation of a fixed copy
- Cost are spread and many become hidden.

8.8 UNIVERSAL DIGITAL LIBRARY (UDL)

UDL or the Universal Digital Library seeks to digitize books of common interest to different Communities of Interest (COI) and make them available in a manner that is independent of language, location and time. A complete solution for this was developed by Carnegie-Mellon University, USA involving state-of-the-art planetary scanners for scanning, cropping, OCR and XML converting.

But the massive efforts and overall costs involved in selecting the books, manpower and hardware make it prohibitively expensive for any one nation to execute the project by itself. Thus it involves the participation of several countries including the USA and China. The Overall International Co-coordinator for this project is Prof. Raj Reddy of CMU and such an international collaboration also ensures that no duplication of efforts is involved while capitalizing on the digital form of the information that can easily be shared and accessed.

The co-coordinator for the Indian effort is Prof N. Balakrishnan, Chairman, Division of Information Sciences and Services at the Indian Institute of Science. Other Indian institutions involved in this project are

- Indian Institute of Science
- CST Mumbai
- IIIT Hyderabad

8.9 VIRTUAL LIBRARIES

Virtual libraries are the new vision of libraries of the future. They are still taking shape in computer and electronic laboratories, but there are some applications that provide an insight of what is coming in the next years. The development of virtual libraries will take place when libraries transform themselves into three dimensional electronic information centres. It will be possible when data storage, data representation and image processing technologies mature to cope with the great amounts of data graphically represented required by virtual information systems.

It's a new concept, the virtual librarian who maintains the virtual library, but it's an important service that librarians and scholars can provide in their fields of specialization. The internet bibliographies will be in effect libraries of critical articles and books selected by the bibliographer. The task of cataloguing literary criticism on the internet at present is not too difficult, because there are not many scholars and scholarly journals publishing on the internet yet. But as more articles appear, there will be a greater need for reliable, selective web bibliographies and web catalogues.

8.9.1 MEANING AND DEFINITION

Digital Libraries and Virtual Libraries are not one and the same. All virtual libraries must, by their very nature, be electronic, but not all electronic libraries are necessarily virtual. A library with all holding on CD-ROMs accessed form stand-alone workstations would be electronic, but it certainly would not be classed as a Virtual library. The key characteristics of a true virtual library are (Sherwell, 1997):

a. There is no corresponding physical collection
b. Documents will be available in electronic format
c. Documents are not stored in any one location
d. Documents can be assessed from any workstation
e. Documents are retrieved and delivered as and when required
f. Effective search and browse facilities are available

A digital library could be (Powell 1994)

- A library with little or no physical presence of books, periodicals, reading space, or support staff, but one that disseminates selective information directly to distributed library customers, usually electronically.
- A more traditional library that has transformed some significant portions of its information delivery channels into electronic format, so that many or most of its customers do not need to visit the library to obtain information.
- A library that operates as a nexus of selected information management activities within the organization, some of them centralized, but most of which happen

through the decentralized staff, resources, and systems and outside suppliers, who are accessible and dispersed throughout the organization.

Whatever a virtual library means, the usage of communication networks and information technology for access, searching and obtaining is a must and this setting does not include printed material except at the output stage. It facilitates personalized service provided on the user's desktop and desktop access to information for end-users changes the way libraries and librarians perform their usual business, i.e. serving their clientele.

The corporate and business libraries are in the forefront to establish and exploit virtual libraries followed by the libraries of Research & Development and academic institutions. For example

1. The National Institute of Standards and Technology, USA developed a virtual library as an intranet.
2. Tilburg University in 1995 started the virtual library with providing electronic access to Tiff images of over 120 journals of Elsevier in economic and social sciences under a license agreement; PDF files of journals from Kluwer Academic and Academic Press were included at the next phase.
3. Boering and Seymour (1996) describe the virtual library and digital image programmes of five educational projects and a problem-based learning series of case studies taken up at the Georgetown University Medical Centre in various disciplines. All these are available on the www.

8.10 INFLUENCE OF INTERNET ON VIRTUAL LIBRARIES

Internet is enabling inter connectivity of computers and computer networks network at global level. Internet is the global network of over 30,000 networks with about 29.7 million host computers spread around the world, dealing with each other through a common set of communication protocols, reaching over 170 countries and providing connectivity to about 75 million users. The growth of Internet has been global and continuous. The subscriber base of the Net is expected to reach 20 million by the turn of the country.

The Internet has changed the notion of a library as a place into a virtual library, i.e. library without wall, shifting the library on to a desktop at the office or home. A variety of technologies are used for accessing the vast electronic information resources available on Internet and the Web. Starting with basic tools like e-mail, and FTP, Internet has shifted to navigation aids like Wide Area Information Servers, Netscape and Gopher; Web clients such as Lynx, Winweb and Cello; and more recently to the consumer-oriented home pages of the Web. Information resources available on the Web are getting inter-linked through Web pages.

8.11 VIRTUAL LIBRARIES AND THE CYBER LAW

Leaving aside technical and other problems to usher in virtual libraries, the most important problem is the copyright in cyberspace. Existing copyright laws have not caught up with the technological developments in cyberspace. Conscious users are confused as to which is right and which is wrong. At present there is no clarity about whether the content of electronic resources on internet is free or priced. Although the copyright statements appear in many cases, they are elusive to locate in some cases. It can be argued that publishers of promotional material, especially advertising and marketing material, on the Web implicitly encourage downloading, print and copying the material for redistribution to more than one in the same organization (Ardito and Eiblum, 1998).

Even if an electronic resource is a free journal or a newspaper, there is no clear cut law whether it is violation to forward the items from them to colleagues, friends or through list serves. Many electronic papers on Internet allow personal and fair use; many more lack explicit statements if it is free or priced. Further, it is a copyright violation to e-mail a Web page by an intermediary to a colleague or a user, strictly for information sake and no financial gain is involved.

Traditional libraries are meeting places of teachers and researchers supporting formal, interdependent and collaborative learning and research. However, virtual libraries facilitate individual, independent and informal learning.

The future of the librarian is inextricably linked with the library and as the role of the library changes so will that of the librarian from custodian to navigator and evaluator of information and information resources, a role that is absolutely crucial in the new Web environment where there are great quantities of information, but finding the quality in the huge haystack is a difficult task.

The librarians in the age of virtual libraries are expected to be

i. Enhanced service providers in a proactive manner
ii. Master of copyright, licensing and electronic redistribution regimes,
iii. Coordinators working with various specialists overseeing information infrastructure, networks and network applications
iv. Skilled organizers of knowledge resources including training of staff and end-users.

So we can say that the traditional library is an ownership environment where as the library of the future is an access environment. The new library of the future should no longer be a physical depository of materials but a 'conceptual gathering' where the actual materials will be dispersed all over the globe and accessed through the electromagnetic media via digital form. A digital revolution contain changes have seen in information field. The changes have resulted into the evolution of libraries into digital libraries.

REFERENCES

1. Berry, JW – Digital Libraries: New Initiatives with Worldwide Implications, *In* 61st IFLA General Conference Proceedings, Istanbul: IFLA, 1995. Booklet, 53-66.
2. Bharadwaj, Pratima – Digital Libraries in New Era, in 3rd Conference of Ranganathan IASLIC Study Circle at BIRD, Lucknow, 2000.
3. DELNET – Advanced Digital Library Resources Centers – Newsletter, Vol. 3(2), December, 1996.
4. Dhaka, RPS & Arora, Kamlesh – Electronic Library, in Annals of Library Science and Documentation, INSDOC, Vol. 42(4), 1995.
5. Feather, Jhon & Sturges, Paul – International Encyclopedia of Information and Library Science, London: Routledge, 1997.
6. Edelson, DC and Gordin, DN – Adapting Digital Libraries for Learners: North-western University: D-Lib Magazine, September 1996.
7. Feldman, Tony – An Introduction to Digital Media, London: Routledge, 1997.
8. Gruyter, L – On the Information Frontier: Virtual Library Could Improve Texans' Access to Knowledge, Texas Libraries, Summer 1993, p.48-50.
9. Kumar, PSG – A Student's Manual of Library and Information Science, Vol.2. Delhi: BR Publ. Cor., 2002
10. Lau, Dr. Jesus – Virtual Libraries: Their Potential for Less Developed Countries, *In* 61st IFLA General Conference – Conference Proceedings – August 20-25, 1995.
11. Lavroff, N – Virtual Reality Playhouse: Explore Artificial Worlds on Your PC, Corte Madera, CA: Waite Group, 1992. p.143.
12. Lyons, Patrice, A – Access to Digital Objects: A Communications Law Strategy; Law Offices of Patrice Lyons, Chartered, Washington, DC. : D-Lib Magazine, October 1995.
13. Malwad, NM ed. – Digital Libraries: Dynamic Storehouse of Digitised Information, New Delhi: New Age International Publishers, 1996.
14. Mambo, B – Virtual Libraries in Africa: A Dream, or a Knight in Shinning Armour, *In* 61st IFLA General Conference Proceedings, Istanbul: IFLA, 1995. Booklet , p.36-41.
15. McClelland, M – Challenges for Service Providers When Importing Metadata in Digital Libraries, University of North Carolina at Chapel Hill: D-Lib Magazine, April 2002.
16. Paul, Glister – Digital Literacy, New York: Wiley Computer Publishing, 1997.
17. Pimentel, K and Teixeira, K – Virtual Reality: Through the New Looking Glass, New York: McGraw-Hill, 1993. p.301.
18. Prasad, ARD – A Digital Library of Library and Information Science: DRTC Bangalore: D-Lib Magazine, November 2003, Vol.9 no.11.
19. Suzie, Allard ed. – Proceeding of the 4th International Conference for Asian Digital Libraries, University of Kentucky, January 2002.

FURTHER READINGS

1. Anthony, LJ, ed. – Handbook of Special Librarianship, London: ASLIB, 1985.
2. Aswal, RS, ed. – Information Networks in India, New Delhi: Ess Ess Publication, 2003.
3. Barna, Arpad and Porat Dan, I – Introduction to Micro Computers and Microprocessors, New York: John Wiley, 1976.
4. Barron, David – Computer Operating Systems for Micros, Minis and Mainframes, London: Chapman, 1971.
5. Baruah, A – Computer Networking in Libraries, Delhi: Kalpaz, 2002.
6. Berry, JW – Digital Libraries: New Initiatives with Worldwide Implications. *In* 61st IFLA General Conference Proceedings, Istanbul: IFLA, 1995. Booklet, 53–66.
7. Black, Uyless, D – Data Communications, Networks and Distributed Processing, New York: Reston, 1986.
8. Blazewritz, Robert, M and Stem, Frank – Microcomputer Systems: Hardware-Software Design, New Jersey: Hayden, 1983.
9. Davis, Gordon, B – Introduction to Computers, New York: McGraw Hill, 1977.
10. DELNET – Advanced Digital Library Resources Centers, New Delhi: DELNET Newsletter, Vol. 3(2) Dec. 1996.
11. Desikan, RS and Muthuswamy, R – Configuring a Local Area Network System for a Technical Information Center: A Case Study, *In* AGLIS Journal, Vol. 8, No. 1–4, 1991.
12. Devdasan, FD – Microcomputer Applications in Library Automation and In–house Information Retrieval, Lucknow: UPLA, Lucknow Librarian – 17(1982).
13. Devrajan, GD and Rahelamma, A V – Library Computerization in India, New Delhi: Ess Ess Publications, 1990.
14. Dewey, Patrick, R– CD–ROMs to Use in Your Library: Description, Evaluation and Practical Advice, New York: American Library Association, 1996.
15. Dhaka, RPS and Arora, Kamlesh – Electronic Library, *In* Annals of Library Science and Documentation, Delhi: INSDOC, Vol. 42(4), 1995.
16. Dubey, Yogendra , P – Computer and Telecommunications Technology: A Statte of the Art *In* Sharma and Ojha, ed. – Advances in Library and Information Science Jaipur:RBSA, 1988.
17. Dyer and Gunson – Directory of Library and Information Retrieval Software for Microcomputers, Aldershot: Gower, 1995.
18. Edelson, DC and Gordin, DN – Adapting Digital Libraries for Learners: Northwestern University: D–Lib Magazine, September 1996.
19. Elashami, AM – Networking CD–ROMs: The Decision Makers Guide to Local Area Network Solutions, New York: American Library Association, 1996.

20. Emery, G – Elements of Computer Science, New Delhi: BPB, 1991.
21. Feather, John and Sturges, Paul – International Encyclopedia of Information and Library Science, London: Routledge, 1997.
22. Feldman, Tony – An Introduction to Digital Media, London: Rutledge, 1997.
23. Gruyter, L – On the Information Frontier: Virtual Library could Improve Texas Access to Knowledge, Texas Libraries, Summer 1993, p.48–50.
24. Haung, Samuel, T – Modem Library Technology and Reference Services, New York: Haworth Press, 1993.
25. Hellerman, H and Conroy, TF – Computer System Performance, New York: McGraw Hill, 1975.
26. Iyengar, TKS – Application of Computers in Housekeeping Operations in Libraries, *In* Parthasarathy, S, ed. Computer Application to Libraries, Information Retrieval and Networking, Bangalore : ISI, 1986.
27. Jackson, AR and Hagarth – Library and Technical Information Services, *In* AS LIB Proceedings Vol. 29(10), p.337–347, Oct. 1977.
28. Jebaraj, Franklin David and Devadoss, Fredrick Robin – Library and Information Networks in India, *In* Library Philosophy and Practice, Vol. 6, No.2 Spring 2004.
29. Jones, Kevin, P and Colin, LM Bell, MORPHS – Mini Computer Operated Retrieval Partially Heuristic System, *In* ASLID Proceedings, 38(3): March 1986.
30. Joslin, EO – Computer Selection, Mass: Addison Wesley, 1968.
31. Kashyap, MM – Database System: Design and Development, New Delhi: Sterling, 1993.
32. Kumar, PSG – A Student's Manual of Library and Information Science, Vol. 2, Delhi: BR Publication, 2002.
33. Lahiri, A, ed. – Library Automation: The Real Crunch, NISSAT Newsletter, Vol. 9, No. 2, 1990. (URL http://www.dsir.nic.in/pubs/itt/nnl9002/nnl9002.pdt).
34. Lancaster, FW – Compatibility Issues Affecting Information Systems and Services, Paris: UNESCO, 1983.
35. Lancaster, FW and Foyer, EG – Information Retrieval Online, California: Melville Publishing Co., 1990.
36. Lasselle and Ramsay – ABC's of IDM PC and Compatibles, New Delhi: BPB, 1990.
37. Lau, Dr. Jesus – Virtual Libraries: Their Potential for Less Developed Countries, *In* 61st IFLA General Conference Proceedings – August 20-25, 1995.
38. Laver, FJM – Introducing Computers, London: FIMSO, 1985.
39. Lavroff, N– Virtual Reality Playhouse: Explore Artificial Worlds on Your PC, *In* Corte Madera, CA: Waite Group, 1992. 143 p.
40. Lewart, Cass – Modern Handbook for the Communicating Professional: New York: Elsevier, 1987.
41. Lucas, A and Nevallo, A, ed. – Encyclopedia of Information Systems and Services, Detroit: Gale Research, 1990.

42. Lyons, Patrice, A – Access to Digital Objects: A Communications Law Strategy; Law Offices of Patrice Lyons, Chartered, Washington, DC: D-Lib Magazine, October 1995.
43. Malwad, NM, ed. – Digital Libraries: Dynamic Storehouse of Digitised Information. New Delhi: New Age International Publication, 1996.
44. Malwad, NM *et al.*, ed. – Digital Libraries: Dynamic Storehouse of Digitized Information, *In* 15th Annual Convention and Conference, 18-20 January, 1996, Bangalore: New Age International Publishers, 1996.
45. Mambo, B – Virtual Libraries in Africa: A Dream, or a Knight in Shinning Armour, *In* 61st IFLA General Conference Proceedings, Istanbul: IFLA, 1995, Booklet, 36-41.
46. Mandal, Mathew – Fundamentals of Digital Computers, New Delhi: Prentice Hall, 1966.
47. Martin, J – Telecommunications and Computer, Englewood Cliffs: Prentice Hall, 1976.
48. McClelland, M – Challenges for Service Providers When Importing Metadata in Digital Libraries, University of North Carolina at Chapel Hill: D-Lib Magazine: April 2002.
49. Murthy, SS, *et al.* ed. – Bibliographic Databases and Networks: Proceedings of the International Conference 1989 / organized by DESIDOC, New Delhi : Tata McGraw Hill, 1990.
50. Nair, R. Raman – Computer Application to Library and Information Services, New Delhi: Ess Ess Publications, 1992.
51. Nilles, Jack, M. – Micros and Modems: Telecommunication with Personal Computers, New York: Reston, 1982.
52. OECD – Evaluation of Computer Systems, Paris, The Author, 1984.
53. Patel, AK and Srivastava, Vishnu – Access to Indian Legal Information Through Internet, Delhi: ILA Bulletin 2006, Vol. 42(3), p.27-32.
54. Paul, Glister – Digital Literacy, New York: Wiley Computer Publishing, 1997.
55. Pimentel, K and Teixeira, K – Virtual Reality: Through the New Looking Glass, New York: McGraw Hill, 1993.
56. Prasad, ARD – A Digital Library of Library and Information Science, DRTC Bangalore: D-Lib Magazine, November 2003, Vol.9 No.11.
57. Rajagopalan, R – You and The Computer, New Delhi: CBI, 1985.
58. Rajaraman, V – Fundamentals of Computers, New Delhi: Prentice Hall, 1985.
59. Rajasekhar, TB – Computer Software for Library and Information Work: Problems and Prospects for Indians, *In* IASLIC Bulletin, Vol. 32, No.4, 1986.
60. Robbins, J – Hard Disk Instant Reference, New Delhi: BPB, 1990.
61. Rorving, ME – Microcomputers and Libraries, New York: Knowledge Industry 1984.

62. Rowley, Jenifer, E – Computers for Libraries, New York: Clive Bingley, 1985.
63. Saffady, William – Introduction to Automation for Libraries, Chicago: ALA, 1989.
64. Salton and Micheal, D – Introduction to Modern Information Retrieval, Auckland: McGraw Hill, 1983.
65. Sanders, Donald – Computers Today, New York: McGraw Hill, 1988.
66. Satyanarayan, NR – Manual of Library Automation and Networking, Lucknow: Royal Book Agency, 2004.
67. Sehgal, RL – Computing & Disk Operating Systems for Libraries, New Delhi: Ess Ess Publications, 1994. ISBN: 81-7000-169-2.
68. Sharma, Pandey, SK – Library Computerization: Theory and Practice, New Delhi: Ess Ess Publication, 1993.
69. Summit, RK – Dialog System *In* Encyclopedia of LIS -Vol.7, New York: Marcel Dekker, 161-9.
70. Suzie, Allard, ed. – Proceeding of the 4th International Conference for Asian Digital Libraries, University of Kentucky, January 2002.
71. Tannenbaum, AS – Computer Networks, New Delhi: Prentice Hall, 1988.
72. Taube, Mortimer – Computer and Common Sense, Columbia University, 1961.
73. Tripathi, SM – Documentation and Information Services and Networks, Vol. 2, Information Systems and Networks, Agra: YK Publishers, 1997.
74. Valauskas, Edward, J and John, Nancy, R, ed. – Internet Initiative: Libraries Providing Internet Services and How They Plan, Pay and Manage, New York: American Library Association, 1995.
75. Vasistha, CP, ed.– Computerisation and Library Network (Seminar papers 36th All India Library Conference, University of Jodhpur), Delhi: Indian Library Association, 1989.
76. Verma, R – Guide to Successful Computerization, New Delhi: BPB, 1990.
77. Wills and Miller – Computers for Everybody, New Delhi: BPB, 1990.
78. Woods, Lawrence, A and Pope, Nolan, F – Librarians Guide to Microcomputer Technology and Application, New York: Knowledge Industry, 1983.

INDEX

P

R

S

T

U

V

W

❑❑❑